Luminous Reality

THE POETRY OF JORGE GUILLÉN

University of Oklahoma Press : Norman

Luminous Reality

THE POETRY OF JORGE GUILLÉN

Edited by

IVAR IVASK and JUAN MARICHAL

LIBRARY OF CONGRESS CATALOG CARD NUMBER: 69–10627

Copyright 1969 by the University of Oklahoma Press, Publishing Division of the University. Composed and printed at Norman, Oklahoma, U.S.A., by the University of Oklahoma Press. First edition.

Brindis

Hijo de la madre Europa,
América hospitalaria,
Por ti levanto mi copa.
Desde el más desnudo paria
De algún país devastado
Hasta el altivo emigrado
Fuera de patria en acoso,
¡Cuántos dan a su aventura,
América tan futura,
Forma de esfuerzo dichoso!

Jorge Guillén

The Impulse Toward Form

by Ivar Ivask

Todo me obliga a ser centro del equilibrio.

Y tanto se da el presente
Que el pie caminante siente
La integridad del planeta.

—Jorge Guillén

I

ANY DISCUSSION of Jorge Guillén should begin with his person, for the Castilian poet is far from being the detached, invisible writer that T. S. Eliot, for example, strove to be. My reaction to Guillén at our first encounter was not one of tongue-tied awe, but of almost exhilarating ease, a feeling of spacious freedom, of being accepted without any diminution of my own self. No polite pretense, no protective mask was needed. It is not surprising that I was, and still am, buoyed up at every new reading of his poetry in which life and art coalesce and verse cadence captures so well the actual inflections of the poet's voice. Listening to him, I could sense Castile, Paris, and Italy as the decisive influences that had shaped his life. A Mediterranean spirit. Yet as the Mediterranean communicates with all the other seas of the world, so Jorge Guillén belongs equally to South America and North America, where he found asylum from 1938 to 1958. A universal Castilian, Guillén finds the problem of Spain just one among others. While regretting the fact that his native tongue is not spoken around him during his North American exile, Guillén now is able to assert: "Moreover, exile has not been for me a totally alienating experience, because I find anywhere on earth the essential things: air, water, sun, man, human companionship. . . . I have never been able to consider myself completely exiled. I am always in this home country called the planet earth."[1]

These are exemplary words that give us a key to the amplitude of Jorge Guillén's poetry, most of which was written away from his native Spain. His poetry offers us the spectacle of a Castilian who transmutes experiences from a number of countries and cultures into his own idiom. *Poemas de Castilla* (1968) and a *Suite italienne* (1964 and 1968) have been extracted from his books, and there is enough material for a *Suite française* and *Suite américaine*. The curiosity and power of absorption are almost limitless in the case of this poet whose claim that the planet earth is his home is no mere rhetorical flourish. Guillén has achieved this range through an unflagging spiritual self-discipline, which has led him from *Cántico* (containing poems written 1919–49) to *Clamor* (written 1949–62) and *Homenaje* (mainly written 1949–66) until he can survey the earth from the plateau of his life-work, which he has assembled under the title of *Aire Nuestro* (1968). *Aire Nuestro* sounds as encompassing as the Roman *mare nostrum,* and it was meant to. Jorge Guillén is the poet of planetary consciousness. From the very beginning this has been perhaps the deepest impulse informing his poetry.

II

In 1966 Jorge Guillén witnessed the chaos wrought upon Florence by the Arno, swollen with torrential autumn rains. His answer to this wild challenge of the elements was two poems entitled *Impulso hacia forma,* which now introduce his *Suite italienne,* magnificently printed by the Officina Bodoni in

---

[1] Claude Couffon, *Dos encuentros con Jorge Guillén* (Paris, 1963), 14; my translation.

Verona to mark the poet's seventy-fifth birthday; the unique homage of a great Spanish poet to Italy is reciprocated in the most fitting manner by a leading Italian press. Guillén saw the Florentine disaster as an attempt upon his very life and all it stood for. The poems are, therefore, more than another token of gratitude toward Italy; they are the latest formulation of the poet's *ars poetica,* which coincides with the fundamental ethical attitude underlying his life and thought. Here are the two last stanzas of *Impulso hacia forma:*

> Lloran junto a los ríos,
> Mientras de aquellos sauces penden mudas las cítaras,
> Los siempre tan dispuestos
> Al abandono de esta terca empresa
> Que es nuestro convivir, todo inventado.

> Italia
> Crea y nos tiende en alto su hermosura
> Junto a ríos de orillas implacables
> En su impulso hacia forma.
> Italia: maravilla sin cesar reanudada.

The Arno can but fulfill the laws of nature (or the wrath of an Old Testament Yahweh) by confronting the beautiful city with the lure of chaos. Two reactions are possible to such a challenge: either the abandonment of the precarious human enterprise, which for Guillén entails continued inventiveness for the sake of our ordered living together, or a renewal of the marvelous impulse toward form, right on the banks of churning chaos. It is clear which solution appeals to the Castilian poet. Just as Florence keeps emerging in its old and renewed splendor from the flood, so Guillén's *Aire Nuestro* represents a similar cosmos born out of years of civil war, exile, world war, and personal loss. Guillén has actually been reproached by critics for his serene vitality, his poetically registered moments of happiness, and his inner balance unshaken by outer earthquakes, as if the faultfinders thought that the classical form and over-all equilibrium achieved in his poetry were a free gift, the work of a naïve person, blind to the numerous ills and injustices besetting our century. Chaos laps around each of his structured books like the Arno at the embankments of Florence. But does the existence of absurdity and chaos absolve man from seeking order, form, and ultimate affirmation of what are real, realized humane values? No, replies Guillén, who stands with a minority of modern poets. The majority seems to prefer to negate, vociferate, lament, and blaspheme, hence only confirming the reader in his hopeless perplexity. Guillén's praise, his affirmation are directed toward the things which are worthy of praise and affirmation—love, friendship, children, art, moments of serenity and fulfillment. Once, sitting in an armchair, the poet experienced such a blessed instant and exclaimed, "The world is well made." His unimaginative critics never forgot that utterance but made it into the central tenet of Guillén's philosophy. If one ignores all the statements made in Guillén's poetry lamenting the imperfections of mankind, history, society, and, as can be seen in the recent Florence poems, even nature, then, yes, the formula, *"El mundo está bien hecho,"* could be indicative of moral obtuseness. This, however, is not the case.

We may ask, why does Guillén gather in his books more moments of happy fulfillment than expressions of futility and depression? Such a question can be answered only with a pointed counterquestion: why should only those poets be authentically modern who bear witness to chaos chaotically? Cannot a struggle with chaos and occasional victories over futility be equally authentic? Like a wise physician, Jorge Guillén offers the poisoned organism an effective antitoxin, not more of the same. Night and chaos are for him only points of departure. Incessantly deluged with the mercilessly honest analyses of a sordid reality by the socially engaged poets, we may lose sight of the humane values toward which we supposedly should be striving. Guillén believes in confronting the contemporary reader with an embodiment of these values in his poetry, rather than lamenting their absence. At the same time he is under no illusion about the rarity of these values in our world. Yet miracles do occur: Florence emerges, again splendid, from the mud; Venice may be like an artificial fireworks above the water, but that fireworks paradoxically endures; a Mediterranean palace descends step by step into the very sea, but precisely this imaginative daring wins out. History is presented in both its creative and its destructive aspects. Besides the evil mediocrity of all dictatorships, as given expression in the scathing poem *Potencia de Pérez,* we find verses in praise of the reconstruction of Rotterdam. Such victories of justice, such joyful celebrations of light take place within the historical, social dimension, not outside of it. They come out of a chiaroscuro of ambiguous shadows which accompanies all of *Aire Nuestro* and even competes for center stage in *Clamor/Tiempo de Historia.* Guillén's poetry fully acknowledges the brutal reality of chaos; his love is bestowed on the impulse toward form wherever it is realized.

Perhaps Guillén is not so much a classicist of the past or a post-symbolist of the present as a visionary of the future. In accepting the *Grand Prix International de Poésie* 1961, the Spanish poet spoke about *Poésie intégrale* with a view to coming developments:

Our epoch takes pleasure, moreover, in plumbing the depths of crises, their problems and anguish. (But has there ever been a century without crises?) Thus our state of mind is summed up in the new imperative: feel anxiety! These last years have given us all numerous occasions to be afraid and to tremble openly. All the same, literary trembling has become the fashion . . . . Let us not be discouraged. Let us avoid the worst complaisance: surrender to the apocalypse. Our planet is quietly traversing a period of astounding growth. The masses of all colors are beginning to become human, and the regenerative forces are ceaselessly multiplying the extraordinary power of man, whose base possibilities are only comparable to his sublime gifts.

For such an expanding human world Guillén finds only integral poetry to be adequate:

Integral poetry! We know its source: the whole man with the stirrings of his imagination and feeling. Individual and collective poetry, hymn and elegy, canticle and clamor—in spite of the anathemas of the pedants. The last 150 years of poetry—since Romanticism—have attained an unprecedented intensity of invention, and the bad prophets who believed in the growing contradiction between the world of science and the worlds of poetry have been mistaken. The latter do not go unnoticed.[2]

In the light of this concept of "integral poetry" Guillén's *Aire Nuestro* assumes another dimension: it bears witness to the discovery of new poetic territory.

III

Yo me admiro cuando pienso que la emoción de los músicos

[2] Jorge Guillén, *Courier du Centre International d'Études Poétiques,* (Brussels, 1963), No. 35, pp. 7–8; my translation.

(Bach) se apoya y está envuelta en una perfecta matemática.
Tus poemas tienen (sobre todo las décimas) polos y ecuador.[3]
—FEDERICO GARCÍA LORCA

The astonishing originality of Guillén's vision of the world,
which lends coherence to the body of his work, has struck me
since my first encounter with his work. The intellectual discipline and the classical forms are needed to master an elementary ontological experience that overwhelms the poet in the
four elements and through his five senses. Leafing at random
in Guillén's *Cántico,* it is not hard to come upon corroborating
evidence: *"Respirar es entender"* (4th edition, 485), *"Los ojos
no ven, Saben"* (*ibid.,* 235), *"La atención es un éxtasis"* (*ibid.,*
313), or *"Ser, nada más. Y basta"* (*ibid.,* 17). Hardly an intellectual classicist is revealed in these quotes. Neither a roman-
ticist, since the Castilian poet claims that *"la realidad me inventa"* (*ibid.,* 18), and not the other way around.

Yet, just as one can dwell too much on the dynamic vitality
of Guillén and adduce such parallels as Gerard Manley Hopkins, D. H. Lawrence, Boris Pasternak, and the Greek Odysseus
Elytis, one can also miss Guillén's originality by perpetuating
the legend of the poet as the student of Mallarmé and the trans-
lator of Paul Valéry, the propounder of *poésie pure.* Neither
do I see much to be gained from comparisons between the
crystalline poems of Guillén and the fragments of our reality re-
fracted in cubist painting. On the other hand, the poet himself has repeatedly expressed his great admiration for music
as such and has given the title *Contrapunto final* to one of the
concluding poems of his *Cántico.* A search in this direction
might yield new, pertinent insights.

[3] F. G. Lorca in a letter to Jorge Guillén dated Granada, September 9,
1926. Jorge Guillén, *Federico en persona,* (Milan, 1960), 124.

But what about our poet's possible affinity with modern architecture, a relationship which so far has been overlooked by every commentator? Is not Jorge Guillén more of an architect of words and verse forms than a secret painter or a thwarted composer? Moving into space, breathing air, and bringing space, air, and sky together—are not these the most fundamental impulses sustaining the architectural structure of Guillén's *Aire Nuestro?* The poetry of Jorge Guillén shares indeed with the buildings of, say, the Finn Alvar Aalto and the American Frank Lloyd Wright a number of essential qualities: the same concern for man's individual happiness, spaciousness and luminosity, magnanimous simplicity and natural elegance, the same lack of sentimentality and pathos, a preference for soaring geometry over romantic ornament. Like the architecture of Wright and Aalto, the poetry of Guillén puts man on an equal footing with nature by subtly harmonizing the two, *"Soy como mi ventana. Me maravilla el aire"* (*Cántico* IV, 145). Balance, equilibrium between man and the world, the inner and the outer, the mind and the senses, is in fact the key to Jorge Guillén's concept of reality. Yet neither the modern architect nor the Spanish poet is afraid of all the changes and innovations that inevitably come with the advance of technology. In a way, a poem by Guillén is as beautifully functional and complete as a window designed by Alvar Aalto. This not only applies to poems that actually do evoke windows in a symbolic manner, such as the above-quoted *Una ventana* from *Cántico* or *Forma en torno* from *Clamor;* it is equally true of his three- to four-line "clover-leaf" miniatures (something between an epigram and a haiku), as well as the longer poems and whole cycles. The collections *Cántico, Clamor,* and *Homenaje,* which now form the monumental *Aire Nuestro,* are like eminently livable buildings of which the individual poem-windows lead the reader into the poetry as much as out of it, back to other men, light, and air. *Aire Nuestro* belongs to everybody who breathes poetry.

IV

El diálogo de Valéry es consigo mismo; *Cántico* es "el diálogo entre el hombre y la creación." La transparencia de Guillén refleja al mundo y su palabra es perpetua voluntad de encarnación.[4]

—OCTAVIO PAZ

Luminous Reality is the first English-language attempt of its scope to chart the whole territory of Guillén's poetry. How did this volume of critical essays come about? What is its prehistory? Herbert Steiner (1892–1965), friend of Valéry and Guillén and editor of the *Collected Works* of Hugo von Hofmannsthal, sent a few copies of his private magazine *Mesa* to a graduate assistant at the University of Minnesota. Engaged in work on a doctoral dissertation about Hofmannsthal, I read some sonnets by Jorge Guillén in Steiner's publication in 1951. *"El son me da un perfil de carne y hueso. / La forma se me vuelve salvavidas. / Hacia una luz mis penas se consumen."* This sent me scurrying to the Spanish stacks of the University library. I well remember the impact Guillén's *Cántico* had upon me: hardly fully understood, it seared through my vague veils of Latin, French, and a minimum of Spanish. To read everything by and about this Spanish poet was the next step, accompanied by more excursions into Spanish grammar.

In 1952 I was foolhardy enough to try to communicate my discovery in an essay written in my native Estonian. The poet

[4] Octavio Paz, "Horas situadas de Jorge Guillén," *Papeles de Son Armadans* (February, 1966), 214 (also included in *Puertas al Campo*, Mexico, 1966).

reacted to an English version of this, my first enthusiastic attempt, with generous kindness. We met at the Modern Language Association gathering in Boston, December 28, 1952, and correspondence, more meetings, and more articles followed. But this is not the place to reminisce. Let it suffice that, as the new editor of *Books Abroad,* it seemed natural to me to dedicate my first issue to "An International Symposium in Honor of Jorge Guillén at 75."[5]

This initial impulse led to other steps. Professor Lowell Dunham, chairman of the Department of Modern Languages in the University of Oklahoma, agreed at once to my suggestion to convene a first "Jorge Guillén Conference" at this university to mark both the seventy-fifth birthday of the Castilian poet and the publication of his *Aire Nuestro* in Milan. It so happened that 1968 also marked forty years since publication of the first edition of *Cántico.* Thus there was more than one reason to celebrate, and celebrate we did. A special committee consisting of Professors Lowell Dunham, James H. Abbott, James P. Artman, Thomas E. Lyon, and I did the planning. The conference took place at the University of Oklahoma in Norman from February 9 to 11, 1968. Twenty-one states of the Union and Canada were represented. There were more than 200 persons at the opening session and 250 for the high point of the conference, a reading by the poet himself.

The six papers of the conference were read by Willis Barnstone (Indiana University, Bloomington), Joaquín Casalduero (University of California, San Diego), Biruté Ciplijauskaité (University of Wisconsin, Madison), Andrew P. Debicki (Grinnell College, Iowa), Ricardo Gullón (University of Texas, Austin), and Concha Zardoya (Indiana University, Bloomington). Professor Juan Marichal (Harvard University) chaired the

[5] *Books Abroad,* Vol. XLII, No. 1 (Winter, 1968).

xvi

panel discussion consisting of the following participants: Ricardo Benavides (University of Utah, Salt Lake City),[6] Manuel Durán (Yale University), Joaquín González Muela (Bryn Mawr College), Luis Lorenzo-Rivero (Carleton University, Canada), Paul R. Olson (Johns Hopkins University), Julian Palley (University of California, Irvine), and the young Spanish poet Lázaro Santana (Wesleyan University). The poet was presented with a silver cup at a banquet in his honor. Since there were several other poets attending our conference, a Literary Tea with Concha Zardoya, Joaquín Casalduero, Manuel Durán, and Lázaro Santana reading from their poetry was a natural extension of the conference. Through a fortunate coincidence and the co-operation of the University of Oklahoma Press, the most extensive selection from Guillén's work in English, *Affirmation: A Bilingual Anthology, 1919–1966,* sensitively translated and annotated by Julian Palley, was published when the symposium was held.

American recognition of the Spanish poet's achievement did not end with these three events. Alejandro Finisterre in Mexico agreed to publish the "International Symposium" from *Books Abroad,* the conference papers in their original language, and the homages that arrived too late for consideration in *Books Abroad.* Thanks to then-President George L. Cross of the University of Oklahoma, a generous grant was made so that *Luminous Reality,* an English version of the proceedings, could be published. The book contains the six papers read at the conference and the entire material published in the Winter, 1968, issue of *Books Abroad,* except for the articles by Willis Barnstone, Joaquín Casalduero, Biruté Ciplijauskaité, and Ricardo Gullón, who are represented instead with their longer confer-

---

[6] Benavides took the place of Professor Robert J. Weber (Wesleyan University, Middletown, Conn.), who was unable to attend.

ence papers; a short greeting by Archibald MacLeish was also omitted. For these items, the interested reader will have to turn to the special issue of *Books Abroad*.

The contributions gathered in the present volume are arranged in five sections. The first section offers nine different perspectives upon the whole range of Jorge Guillén's poetry, the method varying from critic to critic. Belgium, France, Italy, Spain, and the United States are represented. The second section proceeds to closer analyses of single poems and three books by Guillén, *Cántico, Clamor,* and *Homenaje.* The personal tributes in section three are fine examples of the short essay. Since poets such as Rafael Alberti and Carlos Bousoño sent dedicatory poems instead of essays to the Guillén Symposium of *Books Abroad,* their works are reprinted in section four along with two more poems by Manuel Durán and Jaime Ferrán, written expressly for the occasion of the Jorge Guillén Conference. Three biobibliographical items conclude this many-faceted critical mosaic entitled *Luminous Reality.*

Not all the articles and papers were originally written in English. The staff of *Books Abroad* is responsible for the English translation of a number of articles. Several members of the Department of Modern Languages at the University of Oklahoma offered their assistance in translating some of the conference papers into English; they are properly acknowledged at the end of the pieces they translated. Biruté Ciplijauskaité and Salvador de Madariaga prepared the translations of their own works. To all these persons the editors extend a cordial thank-you for their generous help.

The combined efforts of a number of dedicated persons made the symposium in *Books Abroad,* the conference, and now this volume possible. Thus the list of grateful indebtedness must be a long one. I hope that the following persons from the University of Oklahoma will forgive me for not singling out the specific contribution of each individual, yet they, too, must certainly be mentioned for their help: President J. Herbert Hollomon (then president-designate); Vice-President Pete K. McCarter; R. Boyd Gunning, executive director of the University of Oklahoma Foundation.

Mrs. Nan C. Gamble was most helpful in organizing the impressive exhibit of Guillén manuscripts, first and rare editions, in the Bizzell Memorial Library concurrently with the conference.

In conclusion, I especially want to thank Professor Juan Marichal, chairman of the Department of Romance Languages at Harvard for his strong support of the Jorge Guillén Conference and his co-editorship of *Luminous Reality*. To quote Guillén's favorite word, *¡Gracias!*

The Spain of Jorge Guillén's Poetry
by JUAN MARICHAL

> Such as the life is, such is the form.
> —SAMUEL TAYLOR COLERIDGE

THERE IS NO DOUBT that the half-century between the publication of Galdós' novel *Fortunata y Jacinta* (1886) and the death of García Lorca (1936) is the second Golden Age of the literature of the Spanish-speaking nations. It is only in those fifty years that the creative level of Garcilaso and Góngora, Cervantes and Quevedo, Lope de Vega and Calderón, has been reached again by such Spaniards and Hispanic Americans as Rubén Darío and Juan Ramón Jiménez (1956 Nobel laureate), Unamuno and Borges, García Lorca and Pablo Neruda, and many others. It is a wider Golden Age than the previous one and not only because it extended from Madrid to Buenos Aires, from the Chilean capital to Seville, from Central America to Granada: it had more intellectual amplitude than the first Spanish Golden Age.

This is not the occasion to justify this assertion, but I would point out that there was a notorious contrast between the artistic and literary splendors of Spain and her almost total absence from the new domains of European science and humanistic research in the hundred years following the Lepanto victory (1571) over the Ottomans; because if Picasso and Falla have their predecessors in Velázquez and Victoria, if García Lorca and Pablo Casals can trace their ancestry to Lope de Vega and Francisco Salinas, Santiago Ramón y Cajal, the Nobel Prize winner of 1906, could not find much of a Spanish genealogy for his histological discoveries. I would also maintain that post–1898 Spanish humanistic creativity is without a national parallel in the seventy years after the death of Philip II (1598): in short, the world-wide significance of Miguel de Unamuno and José Ortega y Gasset is unmatched in the six "golden" decades of the Age of Velázquez (1599–1660). I should add that Ortega's splendid generation, the generation of 1914—Picasso, Juan Ramón Jiménez, Pablo Casals, Salvador de Madariaga, Manuel Azaña, Américo Castro, Juan Negrín, Pedro Salinas, Jorge Guillén, and Joan Miró—does not have an equivalent in the intellectual history of the Spanish-speaking nations. It was indeed the first generation of Spaniards whose accomplishments in domains as distant as physiology and philology were up to par beyond the Pyrenees.

On the other hand, in the last thirty years—from the Spanish Civil War (1936–39) to the present—many readers outside the linguistic frontiers of Spanish have become acquainted with the writings of a great poet of the generation of 1931: Federico García Lorca. I would even venture to say that for many men and women of our own days Spanish literature is reduced to two names, Cervantes and Lorca: the latter has indeed become the essence, for those not familiar with the Spanish language, of literature in Spanish. Of course, Lorca is one of the tragic symbols of our very cruel age: the sacrificial nature of his death made him so and thus contributed to the spread of his literary reputation outside the Spanish-speaking lands. But, though there is no possible uncertainty about the enormous loss suffered by the literature of Spain and Hispanic America when he was murdered in Granada in 1936, Lorca's appeal to so many readers reveals an attitude not strictly related to the symbolism of his death. His poems about Andalusia and gypsies fit perfectly into the general image left by the Romantics of Spain and things Hispanic. Lorca himself was aware of this factor in his success: "I am getting tired of my Gypsy myth," he wrote to Jorge Guillén (January, 1927). He felt that many of his admirers were falsifying his life and the character of his poetry: "I feel as if they were throwing chains on me," he concluded. But, in spite of his precautions, Lorca could not stop his readers from seeing in his work that Andalusian mirage which English tourists and French writers have never failed to encounter in their travels, or, rather, in their pilgrimages, to southern Spain since the 1780's. What has been called in Spanish *"la España de Carmen"*—that is, the operatic Andalusia of Prosper Mérimée and Georges Bizet—is actually what Lorca's admirers look for and find (rightly or not) in his poetry and drama. Thus, paradoxically, the local intensity of his lyrical "mask" has made Lorca the best-known Andalusian of the last three centuries, and, Picasso excepted, the most universal of all contemporary Spaniards. In a word, by seeming to be true to *Carmen*'s Spain, Lorca became, after Cervantes, the literary face of Spain.

To say now that the direction of intellectual life in Spain since the turn of the century has been a consistent effort to break away from all localisms might sound like an arbitrary debunking of the Lorca cult. But already in 1892 Rubén Darío spoke of the "universalization of the Spanish mind" as the most striking singularity of the "new" Spain. And when Unamuno said a few years later that Spaniards had to search for Man within themselves—*"Buscar al hombre dentro de nosotros"*—he was actually calling on his fellow Spaniards to come out of provincial irresponsibility toward themselves and their country by attempting to offer a Spanish-centered view of life and history meaningful for men of other nations and times. It is true that an outstanding pre-Unamunian group (the so-called Krausists) had made enormous efforts since the 1850's to impart to Spaniards a transcendental sense of life—and in some measure Unamuno could be called their most powerful echo—but those admirable teachers were intent on making the Spaniards lower their quixotic aims and thus become modest but productive Europeans. Unamuno's call for universality of approach and Giner de los Ríos' daily lesson in self-improvement were heard by that generation of 1914 whose work in the arts and the sciences gave Spain the stupendous flowering of the two ante-bellum decades (1916–36).

Though not destroyed as was Lorca's generation (the generation of 1931 went to the field of battle in 1936–39 and became literally a "lost generation" for Spanish intellectual history) the generation of 1914 was also marked by the tragedy of Spain. Some of its most representative men are what André Malraux (speaking of Barrès) has called *"des hautes valeurs amputées"*: a sort of amputation is quite visible in their intellectual trajectories. In a few cases the terminating year is self-explanatory (1936, 1940); in others exile or isolation inside Spain resulted in prolonged silence; but in many (including those whose lives were cut short by the violence of 1936 or by the grief of the post–1939 European collapse) a premonition of insurmountable barriers—perhaps as much within as outside themselves—is seen from their first pages or public actions. Even Ortega shows this discontinuity of the creative impulsion: he once said that the Spaniard's worst inner foe was national despair, and he probably was speaking "through his wounds," as it is said in colloquial Spanish.

Jorge Guillén is thus one of the few members of the generation of 1914 who has been able to reach the aims of his young years. Vigny's saying—*"Une grande vie c'est une pensée*

de la jeunesse réalisée par l'âge mûr"—is entirely applicable
to Guillén's lifework, and not only because he has had the grace
of chronology. I would submit that the creative strength of
Jorge Guillén comes from his fidelity to the original temper of
the generation of 1914. Being a *guillenista* of long standing,
though in the underground, I assume some of my colleagues
will not take it as coming from a hostile camp if I suggest that
Cántico—notwithstanding the poet's own claim of its extra-
temporal character—is in history, is indeed history. Recalling
Georges Bataille's criticism of the famous Sartrian piece on
Baudelaire—*"des choix analogues à celui de Baudelaire selon
Sartre étaient possibles en d'autres temps"*—I would maintain
that Jorge Guillén's song to the plenitude of human life, if possible in other times, would not have been this particular *Cántico*,
this book *muy siglo XX,* to put it in Orteguian terms. This is
because the totality of Guillén's poetry has a deep *"sustentación
de patria"* ("sustentation of [provided by] the fatherland," [*Luz
natal, Cántico*]), that "fatherland" of post–1898 Spain, where
Unamuno's high universal aspirations and Giner de los Ríos'
antiquixotic exigencies became simultaneous motivations for
young Spaniards. *Patria* ("fatherland") has in *Cántico* a direct,
almost literal meaning: the poet's father, Don Julio Guillén, was
one of those dynamic Castilian patricians who contributed con-
siderably with their bourgeois entrepreneurship to that new
Spain of the generation of 1914. Perhaps I should add that, in
contrast to so many others in the Spanish-speaking lands, it
was not a parricidal nor a Cainite (using Unamuno's neo-
logism) generation.

All of this—without forgetting the rejection by the generation of 1914 of the traditional mortuary manners and obsessions of Spaniards—would not be sufficient to explain the
uniqueness of an outstanding creator such as Jorge Guillén.

Mallarmé's reply to the verbal clumsiness of his friend Degas comes perennially to the point: Guillén's poetic achievement springs primarily from his creative handling of words, and *Luminous Reality* attests precisely the international artistic eminence of the Castilian poet. But I know that Don Jorge will not mind having the reader's attention called to the generation of 1914 and the second Golden Age of his Spain.

Ortega's insistence on the meaning of circumstances should justify now a reference to an apparently superficial aspect of the Guillén Conference, held at the University of Oklahoma in February, 1968. All of the speakers and panelists and most of the out-of-town participants on arriving in Norman saw on a motor hotel marquee a rather peculiar sign in the America of the motels: "Welcome Guillén Conference!" That in the night of the Oklahoma plains the name of a Castilian poet should be seen by many local and traveling motorists, who were certainly unaware of the singularity of that motel sign, seemed to be in itself a small concordant note with the lifelong aims of the Spaniard to whom we were going to pay homage and whose work was to be discussed the two following days; the writing of poetry was, after all, a normal activity and deserving of conventional publicity. It should be added that some of us felt that the glow of Guillén's name on that night in the Southwestern plains, so distant from the Castilian plateau of his birth, was also in consonance with the readiness of the poet to feel (and create) at home in any of the Euro-American lands. But that sign of welcome and, even more, the conference to begin the next morning, made us aware of the planetary consciousness of our days: Unamuno's call to universality was visible, too, in that Oklahoma night. "*La realidad proponía un sueño.*"

Contents

II. Analyses of Specific Works

III. Personal Tributes

IV. Poems in Homage

V. Appendix

Illustrations

xxix

PERSPECTIVES
I

The Voice of the Poet:
Aire Nuestro
by Joaquín Casalduero

We have come to pay tribute to *Aire Nuestro,* a work now complete, and to voice the admiration and appreciation we feel for its creator, Jorge Guillén. His work certainly has not ended, and we hope that the day when he ceases to write is still in the distant future.

Aire Nuestro begins with a great affirmation, a great joy, an extraordinary feeling of assurance, which is the result of discovering reality, being, and existence in relation to the world and mankind, an association based on a genuine love for humanity. This world, so deeply human and so pure, in accord with its epoch, offers us a view very different from that of the nineteenth century from romanticism to impressionism. Its most important characteristic is that it places a new emphasis on man on earth.

The first movement is *Cántico,* which has passed through four stages: 1919–28, 1928–36, 1936–45, 1945–50. There are not four *Cántico*s, but one *Cántico,* an organic development which, in addition to its clarity and definite direction, gives us an unforeseen variety, an infinite reality. It is a prodigy of integration: all the variety of the cosmos within the unity which holds it. This fresh objectivity (with nothing positivistic), this new idealism (with nothing Platonic), this phenomenalistic existentialism is expressed with a completely original melody.

3

Those who thought that the world of *Cántico* was abstract did not have an ear for the new music which Jorge Guillén was creating; thus the *décimas* were easily imposed, although their rhythmic clarity and fullness, which create such a pure profile, make Guillenian form and sound somewhat different from the traditional stanza.

The *Cántico* of 1950 is a totality, complete, which does not mean that in its four stages, if we read them separately, we do not perceive all the difference between the slender stem and the robust trunk with its rich foliage. Those who read the four editions are struck first of all by the span of time necessary for *Cántico* to grow, to take form, to develop. The thought reflected in the first *Cántico* is pure impulse, while in 1950 impulse has been replaced by meditation. From the exaltation of 1928, following the same line of thought, we reach the fulfillment of 1936. Beginning in that year, historical catastrophes accumulate rapidly; personal suffering and sorrow also make themselves felt. The years bring with them honors, fame, and maturity, but the architecture of *Cántico* remains unshaken and unbroken. All elements alien to joy, exaltation, and affirmation are admitted into *Cántico,* but they are kept in a subordinate position. The poet himself has said that they are the chorus, the accompaniment to the act of love and order. Destruction is dominated by creation. In the first two periods of *Cántico* the protagonist moves in both a physical and a metaphysical world. His outlook reaches to things and returns to the soul, a body and soul inconceivable without one another and in such complete unity that social and moral elements are not discernible. The dimensions of *Cántico* go from awakening to sleeping, rejecting dreams, or death, for when the poet refers to death, he sees it only as a law of gravitation, as an end.

In the first two editions of *Cántico* we find only one condition, that of the joyful man, the protagonist who in *El Argu-mento de la obra* is called the actor, the man in love. What distinguishes him is not so much his joy as his living fully in the here and now. Past and future are unimaginable without their intimate relationship with the present; as distant, starry spaces are closely united to the present, this here and this now are always the center for this actor, this man in love, who lives in a well-made world, according to the beautiful, but incomprehensibly misunderstood, verse of Jorge Guillén. I do not know why the poet has made so many efforts to explain his concept. "The world is not well made"—I would never use this idea of Rousseau's to establish a similarity between, but rather to mark the difference in the personalities of the Genevan and the Valladolidian. When Guillén says of the protagonist of *Cántico,* "this actor would be nothing removed from his setting," how can a Spaniard not recall *El gran teatro del Mundo?* And when he is bound between awakening and sleeping, how can he not remember Segismundo? Rousseau and the Spanish seventeenth century can be an interesting historical exercise only if we use them to differentiate and emphasize the essentially twentieth-century qualities of *Cántico,* of the exaltation of concrete reality and of existence in this world, of a love so tangible that it rejects all mysticism.

Más allá and *Salvación de la primavera* are two great poetic extremes of Guillén's first period. Their resoluteness, their aplomb, and their sound are the great creation of Spanish poetry of the thirties. We should not, therefore, forget the great effect of elegant simplicity and shimmering transparency of *Primavera delgada:*

> Cuando el espacio, sin perfil, resume
>   Con una nube

5

Su vasta indecisión a la deriva . . .
    ¿Dónde la orilla?
Mientras el río con el rumbo en curva
    Se perpetúa
Buscando sesgo a sesgo dibujante,
    Su desenlace,
Mientras el agua, duramente verde,
    Niega sus peces
Bajo el profundo equívoco reflejo
    De un aire trémulo . . .
Cuando conduce la mañana, lentas,
    Sus alamedas
Gracias a las estelas vibradoras
    Entre las frondas,
A favor del avance sinuoso
    Que pone en coro
La ondulación suavísima del cielo
    Sobre su viento
Con el curso tan ágil de las pompas,
    Que agudas bogan . . .
¡Primavera delgada entre los remos
    De los barqueros!

or the concept of time and space captured in a dimension which succeeds in mythically crystallizing infancy in *Los jardines*:

Tiempo en profundidad: está en jardines.
Mira cómo se posa. Ya se ahonda.
Ya es tuyo su interior. ¡Qué trasparencia
De muchas tardes, para siempre juntas!
Sí, tu niñez: ya fábula de fuentes.

The capacity for creating myth, as in *El Manantial*, makes *Cántico* unique in its time:

6

Mirad bien. ¡Ahora!
Blancuras en curva
Triunfalmente una,
¡Frescor hacia forma!

Guían su equilibrio
Por entre el tumulto
Pródigo, futuro,
De un caos ya vivo.

El agua, desnuda,
Se desnuda más,
¡Más, más, más! carnal,
Se ahonda, se apura.

¡Más, más! por fin . . . ¡Viva!
Manantial, doncella:
Escorzo de piernas,
Tornasol de guijas.

Y emerge, compacta
Del río que pudo
Ser, esbelto y curvo,
Toda la muchacha.

Cántico is poetry of a vital affirmation. This direct line reaches the fullness of *Más allá* and *Salvación de la primavera;* fortunately for the poet, with the passing of time and events, the affirmation is surrounded by a series of negations enabling Guillén, in the last two editions of the confrontation of creative spirit and destruction, to succeed in enriching his voice with a series of registers which in 1928 and 1936 could not even have been expected. His voice becomes heavier, his tone more imperative; it is no longer sufficient to accept status or being. The relationship becomes a conflict, and the ego of *Cántico* confronts sorrow, disorder, and death face to face. This ego, this existence, labyrinthine and agonizing, is quite different from the impressionistic ego.

The first movement of *Aire Nuestro* has a joyful assurance at the beginning and the will to impose its faith and hope at the end. The second movement has never been presented in one volume. This is one difference between *Cántico* and *Clamor*. The first unity is followed by *Maremágnum, Que van a dar en la mar,* and *A la altura de las circunstancias. Cántico* is always a confrontation with reality to arrive at existence. The cadence of *Clamor* is at first one of great agitation, then the adagio becomes more impassioned, and finally it departs from the elegiac and nostalgic rhythm only to return to the first stage of agitation in an attempt to keep afloat, to not go under.

Since 1936, there has been no responsible person who has not tried to remain above circumstance; our tragedy is that we cannot be "*a la altura de las circunstancias,*" either. It is sufficient if we succeed in grasping something to prevent us from being dragged into the whirlpool which seems about to destroy us at every moment. Jorge Guillén has saved himself with his will to live, his hope, and his faith. *Cántico,* after the third edition, receives a subtitle, *Fe de vida,* and then must admit injustice and disorder, sickness and death. So much negation clashes with that faith in life, in order and in creation, in the order of creation.

Clamor, from its first appearance, is accompanied by a subtitle, *Tiempo de Historia.* On another occasion I have explained the idealism of *Cántico* and its epoch as I explained what we are to understand by pure poetry. It will not be difficult for the future student of Guillén's poetry to explain this *tiempo* and this *historia,* to explain how Jorge Guillén approaches history, how he perceives history and time; the student will surely remind us of the "absolute present" of *Cántico,* which is related and so similar to that of Gabriel Miró. The future scholar will cite these lines of 1928:

¡Bodas
Tardías con la historia
Que desamé a diario!

Clamor is the dike which attempts to hold back the flood, to channel its waters from the perspective of *Cántico,* existence, and dignity and clarity of life. Thus the melody of *Cántico* makes a frequent appearance in the purposefully prosaic verse of *Clamor.* Guillén, who turns to proselike verse, also writes prose worthy of a poet. Jorge Guillén's syntax, although very personal, actually offers no difficulty; his vocabulary, as in *Cántico,* has a great treasure of literary words created in the sixteenth and seventeenth centuries. There is also a persistence of the symbolist tendencies of his formative years, which forces him to draw away from primary experience, the point of departure of his poem. This hermetic quality of *Cántico* at times allows us to penetrate more deeply into Guillén's essentially poetic world. In *Clamor,* on the other hand, if we do not know the anecdote or if it escapes us, an understanding of the poem is lost because we have to depend to a great extent upon the allusions to reality. The author himself has warned us that in this period of his work there is an abundance of narration and description. One must bear in mind, however, that both are treated with a great sobriety. This economy of poetic devices reminds me at times of Cézanne.

Maremágnum has a Guillenian structure. It begins with awakening and ends with sleeping. Guillén's poetry is always enveloped in early morning and evening light. But now it is an awakening on a train in the coach which is the world, and the poet captures with great precision the stretching of arms and legs aroused from sleep, all this over the clickety-clack of metal and the rhythm of speed. The sun gradually appears and enters the train windows; the sleeper opens his eyes briefly, only to close them again for a moment. The poet neither insists nor describes in great detail; nevertheless, he captures exactly an unpleasant and uncomfortable situation from which he wants to escape quickly. Noise, confusion, *maremágnum,* but Jorge Guillén, his ear, his spirit, can see in this chaotic agitation a harmony no longer certain or possible.

> . . . Y el tren, hacia su meta lanzándose, corriendo,
> —Mirad, escuchad bien—
> Acaba por fundirse en armonía
> Por sumarse puntual, sutil, exacto,
> Al ajuste de fuerzas imperiosas,
> Al rigor de las cosas,
> A su final, superviviente pacto.

The sonnet *Sueño común* closes the volume. Sleep equated with death is a frequent theme in lyric poetry, but it was never presented this way in *Cántico.* We reach the final tercet of this sonnet to hear:

> Cuerpo tendido: todo en paz te mueres
> Negando con tu noche tantos males,
> Rumbo provisional hacia la nada.

The poet emphasizes the provisory character of the traditionally established similarity. To sleep is peace and the oblivion of all the angers and destructive unrest of the world. Furthermore, Jorge Guillén affirms that *"el dormido no es vil."*

Between the awakening on the train and the sleeping of the sonnet, the poet encompasses the lack of order in the world. Let us note first that the humanity of *Maremágnum* dreams, a perspective we do not find in *Cántico*. Sleeping is no longer rest; nor does night exist only for sleep, since there are also those who cannot sleep. It is a way of living, opened up to the idea of being awake for pain, for noise, for physical discomfort, for police or for bandits, or assassins.

Immediately following the great poem *Potencia de Pérez,* a monument of larger-than-natural size giving us all the human pettiness of Pérez, a miserable nobody, and presenting the images of both a totalitarian regime and the dictator, we have in prose the great clamor of *Ruinas con miedo.* It describes the cowardly attack of Nazi and Fascist air power on Ethiopia and on Guernica, Spain. Picasso has pictured this event on his canvas; Guillén has written a magnificent prose piece against the most vile crime that power has committed in the twentieth century, a crime comparable only to such a scientific invention as the gas chambers in the Nazi concentration camps. Guillén finds the two poles, which in *Maremágnum* maintain the center of this modern confusion, in pride, mythicized in Luzbel, and in sodomy. If I interpret correctly, these two poles correspond to the diversion of intelligence and the senses. The poems, *Luzbel desconcertado* and *La Hermosa y los excéntricos,* are the pillars of the book, which is divided into five parts. The last part, *Guerra en la paz,* refers us to Tolstoy and Unamuno. The modern period in history is one of isms, both artistic and political. *"Dogmas y bombas,"* says Guillén in *Aire con época.* In this part, according to the balance of forces in Guillén's composition, we could find a relationship between *Potencia de*

Pérez and *Dolor tras dolor:* the entire city subjected to the shrill siren screech of the ambulance or of the police wagon, the thousand movements of the city's inhabitants, centered for a fleeting moment around the dying or the wounded, the thief or the assassin. Similarly, the wall, stained by the most shameless of men, stands in competition with the vile and obscene destruction of the air forces destroying a city as the Nazi forces did Rotterdam. There are five questions, and the last one, while asking about the peculiarity of those disorders, seems also to be inquiring into the reason for all the present repugnant absurdity:

> ¿Qué vida inconfesable, qué dolor y delirio,
> qué absurdos, qué esperanzas—las últimas—
> están latiendo en esa confidencia de infeliz?

The caricaturist line, satire, moments of happiness, and joyful notes appear in the first volume of *Clamor.* At times the thought, or rather the intent, is too generalized, perhaps hidden, to be fully understood. In general, the epigrammatic expression in stanzas of three or four short lines, which Jorge Guillén with finesse and wit calls *tréboles,* is accurate.

The excited rhythm of *Maremágnum,* in the second volume of *Clamor, . . . Que van a dar en la mar,* is followed by an anguished and full elegiac rhythm. The seven parts into which it is divided are arranged according to the usual structure, awakening and sleeping. The fourth and central part is the elegiac memory. The great, affectionate rhythm is necessarily related to *Salvación de la primavera.* The awakening from so much sorrow—the sorrow and pain of solitude, of the present which has meaning only through the past—that awakening has a cosmic force; it is resurrection, it is Lazarus who returns to earth. Lazarus emerges from his night, from his darkness, from his rest perhaps, impatient to find again the things of daily life. *Huerto de Melibea* is the final night which transcends death, a night endowed with love. Between this emerging from death and going to meet it, we review a whole life of old age and memories: past in two ways. There are also fatigue, oblivion, and sickness; there are memories of infancy and of youth. *Que van a dar en la mar* is an elegy to the death of the loved one, to the eternally alive, to passing time, to the solitude of man, to what he is always awaiting, to passing life. This elegy imposes memory; it is accompanied by sentiment. Here is an affirmation which instead of being vital is an act of the will:

Ay, los ímpetus de mi fe
Declinan ante el gran enredo.

The will is, in turn, a vital act:

Vivir es algo más que un ir muriendo.

And in another line:

Respiro, no agonizo, vivo y vivo.

In this elegy there are no tears, no sighs, and even less hopelessness. Compared to Espronceda's tragic elegy, Guillén's is a serene, mature, virile acceptance of life as it is, with bright sun veiled at times by a gentle melancholy. This adagio ends, and the third movement of *Clamor, A la altura de las circunstancias,* returns to the fast, excited rhythm of *Maremágnum* but is much more restrained.

13

The composition of the two books is identical: of the five parts, the second and the fourth are the most imposing. The first part is surrounded by the rats of a sinking ship and the rats of the nightmares of an insomniac, a new Hamlet who sees a ghost. Except for the sorrow, the injustice, and the suffering, all is impersonal. The most cruel struggle, the rapidity, the confusion, the passing of time—everything is, for a moment, empty of meaning; everything is, for a moment, useless. There is no overflowing, but the wealth of circumstances, of moral situations, of mankind's interrelationships, of the relation between the earth and the planets and innumerable stars is unrestrained; rather, it would be unrestrained if the feeling of the here and now, of limits, were not constantly present. We do not have to turn to any form of historical classicism, since it is a question of one's own personal environment, of the Being-on-earth. It is very easy to see in the third and fifth parts the pendular polarity in which the world is caught: *El lío de los líos* (superlative) and *A oscuras, Nada más,* and *Nada menos.* The same feeling is evident in the first part: *Despertar español* and *La sangre al río* (instead of *"no llegará al río"*) and *Pietá* and *Cita.*

Let us note especially that the *tréboles,* like the *décimas* at times, or that variation of the ten eight-syllable lines in assonance are a kind of instantaneous lyric, penetrating and forceful, ingenious, brilliant, frequently filled with good humor, a topic not yet studied in Guillén's poetry. Some *tréboles* are iridescent drops of vital joy, of happiness shared with others. Certainly there are strident noises; there is confusion. Guillén even writes *"caos-caos,"* and the shadows, or more, the darkness, increases. Nevertheless, in the third movement of *Clamor,* harmony succeeds in freeing itself from the calamity. For example, the *décima, Enlace,* shows this independence from disaster:

Siento sed. Mi boca busca
Con una tensión de urgencia
Límpida corriente brusca,
Frescor en su violencia
Que ahonde hasta la raíz
Del ser. Soy así feliz
—Y con hambre. Necesito,
Mundo, lo otro, mi pan,
Tantas cosas que ya están
Tendiendo hacia mí su grito.

If in the midst of the brutal turmoil we can struggle against hopelessness, it is because Guillén has faith in mankind, in the dignity of man.

Dimisión de Sancho is a poem which one must read carefully, with an ear to the sound. The prose qualities are definitely intended. There are lines which in reality are only eleven-syllable phrases. The description is admirable; the reader, however, does not have to linger over it, but sees it as a basis and background of the melody of exultation with which the poet plants existence on the earth. We can be grateful to *Cántico*, for through it the integrity of the individual can be saved from the constant and brutal attacks with which technology and hate attempt to destroy it in the complexity of man's world. The purity and simplicity of the melody are beyond our imagination. Guillén's perfect mastery directs the litany. The wonder of concrete reality was discovered in *Cántico*, and this long period of training leads to the outburst in *Clamor*:

—Heme aquí. Sancho soy.
Aquí, desde este punto
Que es el mío en mi patria, mi universo,
Frente al perenne fondo
Que ante mí se articula

15

Como una Creación.
Soy donde estoy de veras situado:
Un simple acorde justo,
Más allá de la fácil complacencia
Pasiva,
Sin atenerme a lazos pasajeros,
Y dispuesto a la acción que a mí me aguarda,
Aunque siempre abocado a un porvenir
Ignoto.
No armonía arcangélica,
No hermosura celeste
Menos y más; mi ajuste verdadero,
Partícipe del mundo,
Partícula de veras insertada.
Mirando el horizonte
La vista es siempre centro
De círculo.
Soy—gracias a mis límites—
Con fuerza
De perfil y destino,
Con tranquila adhesión.

El universo entonces,
O la divinidad,
Traza en torno el gran círculo perenne
Conmovedor instante.
La criatura acepta:
Humilde criatura.

Maravilla rarísima
De la humildad. ¡Oh Sancho!

Las tentaciones de Antonio is necessarily more complicated.
Let us begin by noting that the poet questions himself about

the identification between the ego which dreams and the dreamed ego. Guillén, who in *Lugar de Lázaro* had already shown his capacity for depicting concrete reality and the incorporeal separately, now in the diabolical temptation, with the degrading transformation, depicts an action and a landscape that remind me of Rousseau *le Douanier;* in the angelical temptation, I can almost assert that Guillén depicts a renaissance landscape. This man emerges triumphant from both temptations. His victory upon awakening from his dream consists in saving his existence as a man. The poem begins and ends with this word. Whether it is on the most elementary and simple level, Sancho, or on the complex and higher level of Antonio, man succeeds in preserving his existence unharmed. The poet persists in not yielding. His negation, his "no," is the "yes" of *Cántico.* It is true that *Clamor* appears in the last two stages of *Cántico* and it was necessarily insinuated. One must point out that *Clamor* is dominated by *Cántico.* The poet himself, not the critic, says:

> Es el día del Señor.
> Suene música sagrada.
> Cántico sobre clamor.

Thus his memory is always in the present:

> Al recuerdo se agarra la existencia
> Con ansiedad de historia convivida.

I find the unity of Guillén's works first in the vital affirmation of existence, then in situating Being in this world, and finally in the salvation of Being from the philosophical, moral, and social adversities of the twentieth century.

To conclude by listening once again to the voice of the poet, it will suffice for me to refer to the last part of *Aire Nuestro, Homenaje*, the volume which has just been published. The portentous architecture of *Aire Nuestro* (1919–66) is crowned with this volume so beautifully published in Milan (All' Insegna del Pesce d'Oro). The subtitle is *Reunión de vidas*. Thus, *Tiempo de Historia* is enclosed between *Fe de vida* and *Reunión de vidas,* and these lives flow together in the life of the poet. It is a life on two levels: first, poetry and general culture and the exercises in translation; later, friendship, a tribute to the friendship which centers around the poets of the generation but which is amply extended. This gigantic current is no longer set within the framework of awakening and sleeping but goes from *El Génesis* to the *Obra Completa*. This trajectory gives us the scale of *Aire Nuestro*. In the execution of his great project the poet has fixed his attention on trivial facts, on small things that always give the exact proportion of the colossal poetic world in which the most concrete things are always found in air and light. It is always the world and in it, mankind.

The center of *Homenaje* is another great love poem, *Amor a Silvia*, which has a line from Tasso as an epigraph. Inserted into the perfect circle of *Aire Nuestro,* there is this triangle of the two love poems and the elegy of love.[1]

Translated from the Spanish by JAMES H. ABBOTT

[1] See also Joaquín Casalduero, *"Lugar de Lázaro," Books Abroad*, Vol. XLII, No. 1 (Winter, 1968), 23–25.

The Greeks, San Juan, and Guillén

by WILLIS BARNSTONE

JORGE GUILLÉN is an absolute poet, seeking to express fundamental laws. As such he is a passionate physicist. To find his
ancestors, we must look back not only to obvious persons—the
poets San Juan, Lope, Fray Luis, and Manrique—those
whom he loves and in part learns from and quotes in his work,
but to those whom he resembles through an affinity of values
and methods. We must return then to the earliest physicists in
the West, the pre-Socratic philosophers, who, like Guillén, were
seeking fundamental principles to relate matter and being. The
pre-Socratic philosophers of science, we may remember, were
concerned with describing the elementary particles—they called
them atoms or breaths of energy—which underlie all matter.
They are in better standing today among philosophers of science
than is all the history of traditional philosophy between them
and now. And how did they express themselves? Normally in
poetry. There are many ironies in the notion that the most scien-
tifically oriented philosophers before the twentieth century were
the only philosophers to resort to poetry as the means of expressing truth. Since then we have had philosophers who wrote
"poetically"—Nietzsche, Bergson, Santayana, even Plato—but
only the earliest Greek atomists, and those Latin philosophers[1]
who imitated them, used poetry to express philosophy.

[1] For example, Lucretius.

The early Greek philosophers, like Guillén, were seeking to connect all things and being in the world. They gave different solutions, and the Milesian, Pythagorean, and Elian schools each had its own logos. Empedocles held that the four basic elements in the world are moved by love and strife. Heraclitus saw an identity of opposites in all things, with fire (energy) as the basic unifying principle. Parmenides, who wrote exclusively in hexameters, saw the unity of thought and being, thus anticipating Descartes. The common element in all the pre-Socratics was their belief in an apprehensible world stuff, a single reality, in which divinity was removed from the gods and found in this common world stuff.[2] The early philosophers were, of course, deprived of later mechanical tools which now permit scientists to examine the substructure of matter. They relied on what could be comprehended by the naked eye, and here too, in a curious way, they were necessarily closer to Guillén, who speaks abstractly about only what can be sensorily understood.

Like the Greeks, Guillén says many things and has one central notion: we are. The "we" includes himself, you, me, things, the world. The creative surprise is in awakening to an awareness of being. His great striving is to make the connection real between himself and all about him. To do this, he begins, *"No soy Narciso."* He affirms, *"No hay soledad. Hay luz entre todos. Soy vuestro"* (*Afirmación,* p. 258). *"Luz nada más."* (*Anillo,* p. 171). An elementary theorem, concurring with the Greek habit of applying abstract logic to concrete objects in life, may be found in these poems. It might read: (1) Light is in me. (2) The same light is in you, in things, in the world. (3) We, with the same light in us, are one and the same.

---

[2] A form of pantheism is evident in Heraclitus' statement, "God is day and night, summer and winter, war and peace, fullness and want." In other pre-Socratics the notion of God is simply all that is.

With this we have moved one step beyond the first central notion of "we are" and conclude "we are one."

Guillén takes this notion of we are and its corollary, we are one, and expresses them in innumerable ways, each time with the authentic voice of accurate experience. At times he appears to follow the course of Heraclitus in speaking of the unity of opposites:

> Nubes por variación
> De azares se insinúan,
> Son, no son, sin cesar
> Aparentes y en busca.
> —*Salvación de la primavera,* v, p. 97

He writes further, *"No soy nadie, no soy nada, / Pero soy— con unos hombres"* (*Cara a cara,* vi, p. 523). There are many ways to reach the being, the *gozo de ser,* which he is celebrating, and if we mention Heraclitus' paradoxes, the affinity is sound; but this is only one of Guillén's many means of statement. With Parmenides there is an equal affinity, which we see in Guillén's repeated equation of thinking and being. Like Parmenides', Guillén's mind and body are one. Parmenides was struck by "an intense consciousness of Reality itself, the sense that *it is,* and the wonder of it."[3]

Guillén is similar to another Greek, Anaximenes, who connected all men and the world through air. Anaximenes records: "First . . . as our soul, being air, holds us together, so do breath and air encompass the whole world." Guillén writes:

> A una creación continua
> —*Soy del aire*—me someto.

[3] A. R. Burn, *A Traveller's History of Greece* (London, Hodder and Stoughton, 1965), 106.

¡Aire en transparencia! Sea
Su señorío supremo.
                    —*El aire,* 513

Furthermore, he confirms that his life is air, air with faith:

Y la vida, sin cesar
Humildemente valiendo,
Callada va por el aire,
Es aire, simple portento.

Vida, vida, nada más
Este soplo que da aliento,
Aliento con una fe:
Sí, lo extraordinario es esto.
                    —*Ibid.,* 510

I have tried to find parallels between the Greeks and Jorge Guillén neither to suggest nor to deny any direct influence upon the poet. The pre-Socratic Greeks, upon first exploring the natural universe, loosed the bacteria of their ideas upon the world, and none of us since can be completely free of their way of thinking. It is rather to show that Guillén, like the early philosopher-physicist-mathematicians, is a poet obsessed with seeking the fundamental laws that explain the cosmos. All other considerations are secondary, in minor print; in *Cántico* secondary poems even have smaller-size titles. Like the early Greeks, Guillén uses poetry to express himself. Like them he uses an exact philosophical vocabulary of abstractions to speak of specific things of the world. It is for these reasons that one may speak of him as an absolute poet, unique in the history of poetic literature. For example, he writes, *"Ser, nada más. Y basta."* The diction of the first three words is philosophical and abstract. The last phrase, *"Y basta,"* is colloquial talk, yet is similarly exact. It terminates the abstraction of *"Ser, nada más,"* and, as so often in his poems, contributes to the climactic tempo of ideas which in Guillén, and in Guillén alone, makes the abstract ecstatic. If Heraclitus used fire to unite the world, Guillén, who does not disown fire, uses all the elements—fire, air, earth, water—and infuses them with faith, with vibrant being. Even his darkness vibrates with enthusiasm. Guillén is the poet of the world living.

To capture in words the alive essence of the "world living," Guillén invented an original poetic language, the language of precise ecstasy. The poet wants a language of *"más verdad,"* so he refines and refines his language till formally no words other than key ones remain. These in turn express no ideas other than the intellectual bone, no emotion other than what has become transformed into fire. Guillén seeks the exactness of truth so passionately that he materializes abstract truth in his search for a precise language: truth rushes toward him and tramples him.

> Y la verdad
> Hacia mí se abalanza, me atropella.
> —*Más verdad,* 354

And he calls for it to come with all its virile fury,

> Venga más sol feroz.

> ¡Más, más verdad!
> —*Ibid.,* 354

Guillén has invented the language of the passionate scientist.

We may now begin to put together a few notions that have been discussed. We have said that Guillén, like the pre-Socratics, is basically concerned with the underlying essence of the cosmos. He discovers that the essence is the same outside and within him. Thus, not only does he awake, with the force of the sun, to his own being, but to that same being in the world. Thereupon he affirms, yes, he is one with that being in the world; be it the whole planet, light, air, a thing, a woman. His connection to that *anillo,* ring, outside him is love; and his energy is directed entirely to that love which joins him and the world. To express all this, like a modern linguist, he invents a new language with its own logical structure and lexicon, and we have called this the language of the passionate scientist.

Can we derive from these notions a further conclusion? Inevitably, we must see a design here and place Guillén with all his originality in a larger pattern. Other poets have attempted, perhaps less happily and without Guillén's absolute rigor, to form some kind of union. Guillén goes further than others in accurately clarifying the labyrinths of his self-realization, but others have also explored similar metaphysical paths. Generally, we call these poets by the very loose and abused term "the mystics." Can such a secular writer as Guillén be considered a mystic—a scientist, as we have called him? For want of a better term, we shall call him just that, a mystic, a secular mystic. This of course makes it obligatory to define the term as we are using it. To do this, it will first be helpful to speak of the other great mystic in Spanish, San Juan de la Cruz, the Spanish poet Guillén most resembles and from whom he derived the title of *Cántico,* the poet we shall also call, in his poetry if not his commentaries, a secular mystic.

The major authority for speaking of San Juan's poetry as secular and not religiously mystical is Guillén himself. To my knowledge he has been virtually the only distinguished reviewer to speak of San Juan's poetry with critical objectivity and to distinguish between the religious mystical process which San Juan's commentaries attribute to his poems and the luminous earthly creations in the poems themselves. Guillén writes:

> This brings us, then, to the conclusion that San Juan de la Cruz, the greatest poet of all the mystics, composed poems which it is customary to consider mystical for reasons that are biographical and allegorical, on the basis of a combined reading of the prose and poetry which superimposes the commentaries on the verses. Our purely poetic reading does not take anything away from the poems, which are indeed poems, and admirable ones, without biography or allegory. Their poetic value is not heightened by being turned toward the conceptual.[4]

And he writes further:

> Strictly speaking, with complete theoretical rigor, they are not, they cannot be mystical. The almost perfect autonomy of the images, so continuously referring to human love, admits neither the evocation of the experience, which is not conceivable or revealable, nor the interposing of thought upheld by allegorical scaffoldings outside the poetic structure.[5]

In these passages cited, Guillén is rejecting San Juan the religious mystic within his poetry as opposed to San Juan the religious mystic in his biography or in his religious commentaries. We shall attempt to show, however, that while the term religious mystic for San Juan of the poems is wrong, the term

[4] Jorge Guillén, *Language and Poetry*, 115.
[5] *Ibid.*, 118.

secular mystic is the appropriate term for both San Juan and Guillén.

The western mystical tradition from which San Juan derives his ideas may be seen in the pre-Socratic, Pythagoras. It was the Pythagoreans among the early Greek philosophers who were concerned with "purification and reincarnation of the soul"; in regard to their number theory and cosmology, they separated the world into the Limited and the Unlimited, the perfectly knowable and the dark and chaotic. The essential dualism of the Pythagorean became in Plato an ultimate separation of soul from body, in later philosophy, the Cartesian split. For Plato in the *Republic* and in *Phaedo* there is an absolute line demarcating the mind and material things. The body and its senses make up a shell from which man must rise in order to attain a knowledge of the Idea of the Good. Pure love then is a departure from the bonds of the body into the luminous world, outside the Cave, to bring the mind into the presence of a spiritual sun. The dualism of mind and body in Plato is developed in Plotinus and the Neoplatonists and becomes in the West the basis for religious mystical thought. Plato's Idea of the Good becomes God. The mystical process of darkness (freeing of mind from matter), illumination, and union with God is the subject of mystical writings, from à Kempis and Eckhart to the religious prose of San Juan and Santa Teresa.

In San Juan a description of the three stages of darkness, illumination, and union is the subject of his commentaries. In the poems the allegory of the mytical process is expressed through the union of lovers. It is here that Guillén denies that the symbolization in the act of the lovers does indeed convey a religious mystical union. To repeat his words: "The almost perfect autonomy of the images, so continuously referring to human love . . ." does not admit "the interposing of thought

upheld by allegorical scaffoldings outside the poetic structure."
What then does the love scene in San Juan convey, how is it
related to Guillén, and how do we derive from all this that
the secular mysticism in San Juan is an analogue of the secular
mysticism in Guillén? To answer these questions, we must examine how San Juan in his poems makes use of the mystical
tradition.

San Juan is a poet of paradox. Like Heraclitus, he believes
that what goes up comes down, what is dark is light; there is a
unity of opposites. In regard to the mystical tradition, he is also
the poet of paradox. Ostensibly he derives from the Platonic tradition, and in his commentaries it is clear that the dark night is
the struggle to leave the flesh behind. *"Estando ya mi casa
sosegada,"* say the commentaries, signifies that when bodily
senses are asleep, the spirit can be detached to see and be one
with God. And we see in Plato how the body is considered a
seat of evil in which the soul is a prisoner. In *Phaedo* he writes:

> While we are in the body, and while the soul is mingled
> with this mass of evil, our desire will not be satisfied, and our
> desire is of the truth. For the body is a source of endless trouble
> to us. . . . moreover, if there is time and an inclination towards
> philosophy, yet the body introduces a turmoil and confusion
> and fear into the course of speculation, and hinders us from
> seeing the truth, and all experience shows that if we would
> have pure knowledge of anything we must be quit of the body,
> and the soul in herself must behold all things in themselves.[6]

San Juan followed the mystics in their flight toward light
and union. His love poems, especially *Noche oscura,* follow
the experience of darkness, light, and union. But while San

[6] Plato, *Phaedo,* translated by B. Jowett (Garden City, New York, Double-
day and Company, Inc., 1961), 498.

27

Juan may have been impelled by the mystical tradition of Pythagorean and Platonic dualism, where the spirit frees itself from the bondage of the evil body in order to have a pure knowledge of the Good in the poems, paradoxically, he achieves quite the opposite goal. If we read what the poems say, rather than what he says they say, San Juan's poems celebrate the love of the full man, not of the incorporeal angel or the soul. As such he is the first Spanish poet of the Golden Age to bring the body fully into the terrain of human love, to depart from the Platonic idealizations of Dante and Petrarch which dominated Renaissance poetry throughout Europe. And as such he most resembles a great love poet of England, John Donne, the first Englishman of the Renaissance who neither transcended sex nor sought detachment from the body, but rather unified body and soul as elements in the full human condition. In poems such as *The Canonization, The Good Morrow, The Sunne Rising,* and *Lovers Infiniteness,* Donne rejoiced in both the physical and spiritual union of man. Donne and San Juan both have the Aristotelian-Thomistic view that love is the act of an animated organism. Aquinas asserts that the soul and body of man are in harmony, rather than in opposition, and that the soul is "capable of its realization only through having a material substance in which to express itself."[7] The Aristotelian view asserts the goodness of the body and its necessary role in the act of love.

In effect, in his attempt to escape from the world and the body, San Juan brings the world and the body into magnificent full focus. Guillén understands perfectly this paradox in San Juan, and in speaking of this in San Juan, he also gives a succinct description of his own poetic credo. He writes:

[7] Charles M. Coffin, *John Donne and the New Philosophy* (New York, The Humanities Press, 1958), 48. Coffin is quoting W. Windelband on Aquinas, from W. Windelband, *A History of Philosophy* (New York, 1898).

San Juan's extraordinary adventure, his fusion with the Absolute, leads him to write, in the most relative and concrete manner, poems of human love—some of the most beautiful the world has known.

And further describing San Juan in a way which handsomely describes his own poetry, Guillén writes:

For his inner life gives rise to the most lofty affirmation of the world and its creatures.... San Juan de la Cruz achieves a poetry that is everything: illumination and perfection.[8]

In these notions of "affirmation of the world and its creations" and poetry which is "illumination and perfection," we may find in San Juan the elements of the secular mystic, which are equally present in Guillén. Both San Juan and Guillén follow the mystic's path from darkness into light and union, psychically if not theologically: San Juan's psychic or secular mysticism is by practice, if not intention, Guillén by clear and full intention. San Juan is more concerned with the union of man with woman, Guillén, of man with the things on and above the planet, including woman and all other things. In San Juan's *Cántico espiritual*, a poem of light, he comes closest to Guillén's *Cántico* in that he celebrates not only man and woman but roaming creatures and nature.

In speaking of Guillén, we originally noted that his first discovery as a poet is that he is, and secondly that he is one with the outside world. In describing his language and obsession in seeking elemental laws of being, we have related him to the protoscientific pre-Socratics who used the language of

---

[8] Guillén, *op. cit.*, 119–21.

poetry to describe the cosmos. In speaking of the three stages of the mystical experience—I am, I see, I am one—we have linked him to San Juan and called them both secular mystics.

Finally, let us examine the nature of his trip to ecstasy. In the very first lines of *Cántico,* Guillén writes:

> (El alma vuelve al cuerpo,
> Se dirige a los ojos
> Y choca.)—¡Luz! Me invade
> Todo mi ser. ¡Asombro!
> —*Más allá,* 16

In the Aristotelian-Thomistic sense, body and soul are joined. And light invades him! The word *asombro,* astonishment, is the poet's word to express the state of blank wonder, which in San Juan is his *"un no saber sabiendo,"* the moment when the mystic remains *balbuciendo,* stammering, before the knowledge of the ineffable. Like San Juan, Guillén does not remain in his shell of being. He puts before him in his typical, most elemental, and primitive way, the task of man: to be more, to join, to reach the circle around him. After awaking to and declaring man's biological solitude, his *"soledad sonora,"* his whole effort, like those early Greeks and San Juan, is to be connected with *the other.* He describes the other—a woman in *Salvación de la primavera*—as part of the world's particles of energy, part of the world stuff:

> Me centro y me realizo
> Tanto a fuerza de dicha
> Que ella y yo por fin somos
> Una misma energía.
> —*Salvación de la primavera,*
> VIII, p. 102

To join her, he does so through love:

> ¡Amar, amar, amar,
> Ser más, ser más aún!
> ¡Amar en el amor,
> Refulgir en la luz!
> —*Salvación de la*
>   *primavera,* v, p. 98

This is the illumination. He is almost wordless, and repeats himself like the babbling secular mystic:

> ¡Tú más aún: tú como
> Tú, sin palabras toda
> Singular, desnudez
> Única, tú, tú, sola!
> —*Salvación de la*
>   *primavera,* ix, p. 103

The two join:

> Y se encarnizan los dos violentos
> En la ternura que los encadena.
> (El regocijo de los elementos
> Torna y retorna a la última arena.)
>   —*Anillo,* iii, p. 172

This moment of perfect union and the thirst to obtain it appear again and again in Guillén. As in San Juan's writings, each time it does, there is a moment of breaking loose, a spiritual and physical orgasm, which is the secular mystic's experience. Guillén's *Llama de amor viva* (San Juan) illuminates the climax of

Gozo de ser: el amante se pasma.
¡Oh derrochado presente inaudito,
Oh realidad en raudal sin fantasma!
Todo es potencia de atónito grito.
—*Anillo*, III, p. 172

The *"atónito grito"* is that instant of total nowness. Before one arrives there, he naturally must pass through dark tension (which may be torrid white).

¡Desamparo tórrido!
La acera de sombra
Palpita con toros
Ocultos. Y topan.
—*El Sediento,* 74

The last phrase *"Y topan"* brings him to a climax. They join. The peak of ecstasy is reached in a wide-awake dream when he drinks the water of love:

¡Ah! Reveladora,
El agua de un éxtasis
A mi sed arroja
La eternidad.—¡Bebe!
—*El Sediento,* 74

In these last few pages I have quoted a few lines here and there to support the theme of Guillén's most primitive obsession with being and with the fire and light that appear when that being joins with things in the world. Like the pre-Socratics and San Juan, Guillén removes divinity from God and delivers it to man. He follows the experience of the mystics in a secular way, leaping from the darkness of solitude into light and union, but his trip from small to larger being, from self to ecstasy, is translated not into the ways of a divine soul and God but into the workings of passion and intellect. No poet, with the possible exception of the early Greek scientists, has used such a naked, philosophically pure language to track that knowledge of the cosmos and to affirm his oneness with that cosmos. No poet, with the possible exception of San Juan, has lived so fully and affirmatively in the felicity of that orgastic union of his being with the lover in this world, now, on this planet, in this cosmos.[9]

[9] See also Willis Barnstone, "Two Poets of Felicity: Traherne and Jorge Guillén," *Books Abroad,* Vol. XLII, No. 1 (Winter, 1968), 14–19.

Una gloria ya madura bajo mi firme decisión

by Biruté Ciplijauskaité

The title of the poem containing this line completes its significance and sums up the attitude of the poet in the totality of his work; *"Al margen de* Las mil y una noches" points to the fact that he sees himself on the threshold of a universe full of possibilities that is asking for his amorous, but at the same time decisive, attention. With the same attitude, the poet was affirming in *Cántico: "Todo, | Todo hacia el poema"* (p. 31). Now, guided by a profound intuition in his heart, he deems it necessary to pronounce only one word, *"¡Sésamo!"* Its magic power, but even more so the poet's full confidence in it, permits him to reap the marvels, not yet defined, of this world. As we reach the last poem of *Homenaje,* we must admit that the adjective "latent" modifying the "mature glory" becomes superfluous: the glory of creating has been fulfilled in the work.

A fervent desire for unity and a precise goal have guided the poet ever since the first poems of *Cántico* started to take shape in his mind.[1] "Every great poetic work consists of relating one element with another, without ever leaving the same place: the Creation," affirms Guillén, praising the poetry of Berceo.[2] From the very first poems on, each line he creates is incorporated into the final project, *Aire Nuestro,* which will

---

[1] Declaration of the poet in the Introduction to *Cántico: A Selection,* 8.
[2] Guillén, *Language and Poetry,* 12, hereafter designated *LP.*

be presented as a perfect architectural figure. In order to achieve his goal, the poet is constantly exercising his "firm decision." *Cántico, Clamor,* and *Homenaje* are permeated with the same will power. Through it, through a relentless effort, art can be seen as a possible glory:

> El deseo despunta, y, ya más alto,
> Adquiere estilo, forma, fortaleza
> Con la concentración de su esperanza.[3]

In order to define it more precisely, one could say that the joyous glory consists of this striving, this creating; it is the process that is important, not the end result. The last line of *Homenaje* confirms it: *"Triste, mi paz: la obra está completa"* (p. 595).[4]

In *Cántico* the poet indicates the main objectives of his work, plenitude of life and plenitude of the poetic word. Even at times of less confidence, admitting that the circumstance does not justify exultation, he maintains this predisposition: *"Deber de plenitud, hombría andante"* (*A*, 137).[5] Thus, when he speaks of Bécquer, he cannot adopt the latter's complaint about the inadequateness of the words. For Guillén poetry means words in which plenitude has been achieved (*LP*, 144). Confidence in finding the exact word makes the act of giving names to all things of the utmost importance: through it, the thing and the person receive their exact place in the universe and become real. The creative act is based on finding the adequate word, which permits the establishment of a lasting con-

---

[3] Guillén, *Homenaje*, 302, hereafter, designated *H*.

[4] We know, however, that the poet will continue to create and to experience the glory of this creating.

[5] *A = A la altura de las circunstancias; C = Cántico; M = Maremágnum; Q = Que van a dar en la mar.*

tact with the universe: *"La palabra y su puente / Me llevan de verdad a la otra orilla"* (*H*, 219). Always, he strives for precision; it is not sufficient to suggest vaguely.

The search for the exact expression, present in all poets of his generation, imposes another necessity, that of putting the words into order, condensing them, extracting their essences. Such poetry cannot be dominated by impulse; even the most spontaneous poet must be aware of the value of precise order. Guillén sees and praises this aspect even in a poet like Lope:

> Aún desde la Corte, mundo estrecho,
> El panorama del vivir atruena
> Los oídos como una batahola
> —Que un hombre, sin embargo,
> Convierte en ritmo y rima.
>
> —*H*, 136

The sublime goal is to create art based on life. The unconscious and the surrealist are considered trivial; incoherence mutilates a work that has been conceived as a unity. At times even in Guillén one perceives a slight echo of Pedro Salinas' *"seguro azar,"* but it is always confined within limits: *"Nadie se resigna al total azar, al Absurdo"* (*H*, 488). Composition and structure are essential companions of emotion; even enthusiasm can be ordered. Architecture appears as one of the great values, and Guillén exalts the value of poets who believed in it: Fray Luis and Góngora. For Guillén poetry in its fullest meaning is the conscious creating of a work of art.

In *Homenaje* the theme of art resurges with great intensity. A major part of the book consists of an homage to the art of others, confirming Guillén's capacity for admiration. Art is presented there as a perfect compenetration of form and content, never as a mere artifice. In *Cántico* the poet affirms: *"La forma se me vuelve salvavidas"* (*H*, 263). In *Language and Poetry*, discussing the ineffable mastery of the great poems of San Juan de la Cruz, he points out that what one admires there is as much inner as outer form, mastery in the most transcendental sense as opposed to empty virtuosity. Form appears there as the most sublime expression of the essence of poetry, the poetic intuition brought to word.

The plenitude of a poetic work can only be achieved if he who creates is not a mere poet, but is, above all, a man, a man in contact with his world. Therefore, when he once was expressing his thought on pure poetry, Guillén said, *"Poesía pura, ma non troppo."* The imperfections of a living being must be admitted; the effort to overcome them is of greatest value. The poet has given the title *Viviendo* to one of his books, underlining the importance of life. He exposes his basic attitude very clearly in the poem that bears the same title, *"Acepto / Mi condición humana"* (*Q*, 86), and repeats it more than once in *Homenaje*, *"Hombre soy. / Me resigno humildemente"* (p. 29). Absolute perfection is not necessary; with his weaknesses, man is more readily recognized as a brother (*H*, 83). To live a man's life is the most essential basis for creating a work of art: only as man and as poet at the same time is he who creates able to find a union between the real and the artistic world.

Conscious creating, bearing in mind not only a perfect form but also a unity of content, imposes certain basic attitudes that can be considered as constants of the poetics of Jorge Guillén. Above all, attention is necessary: to be attentive in his encounters with man, with the world, with the words. Defining *Cántico*, the poet has said that it represents an act of attention (Introduction, *Cántico: A Selection*, 12), complementing this definition in a poem in that book: *"Una atención que llega a ser ternura"* (*C,* 133). The desire to understand and to share what has been understood opens the way to communication and anticipates a similar attitude in the other. This need for communication seems to be increasing as years go by. In *Homenaje* an entire part bears the title *Atenciones;* its motto clarifies the significance:

> La atención multiplica sus miradas
> Curiosas, favorables, amistosas,
> Ya atenciones: obsequios a las cosas
> Y gentes, con más luz realizadas.
> —*H,* 129

He who is attentive is almost always humble. Those who are sufficient to themselves, who have exaggerated confidence in their abilities, do not need the world because they create their own. On the contrary, Guillén can only exist with and in the universe. Always open to an amorous contemplation, through which he captures the essences, he never loses the measure, knowing that even the most insignificant can lead to the sublime. Always he sees himself in relationship to the cosmos:

> Dependo,
> Humilde, fiel, desnudo,
> De la tierra y el cielo.
> —*C,* 73

Explaining the essence of Berceo's poetry, Guillén admires his modesty and humility. Inspired by this same feeling of humility, Guillén himself so often exclaims, *"¡gracias!",* recognizing that every achievement is almost a miracle. Throughout the three parts of *Aire Nuestro* the condemnation of Narcissus

is evident. This does not mean that the poet does not contemplate himself; he does so, but he never pretends to be the
only one, although often his position is a central one. This
theme appears in *Cántico;* in *Homenaje,* it is defined more
exactly:

> He de otear y descubrir el orbe.
> Desde mi cárcel, "yo," frente a la anchura,
> Soy diminuto centro que la absorbe.
>
> —*H,* 341

The conscience of exact proportions influences his concept
of the relationship between poet and poetry. Even the most
conscious and most desirous of perfection, the one who most
closely approaches the plenitude of the poetic work, admits
that he feels subordinated to a supreme power and is conscious
of the fact that his work has been possible only with the help
of superior forces:

> ¿Yo en marfil con su lunería?
> Ese hombre que se despierta
> No es el autor con su apellido.
> Tú eres, es tu acción más cierta,
> Cada mañana la has vivido.
> Poesía a todos abierta:
> Poesía.
>
> —*H,* 493

The attention of one who is humble is the source of the
most admirable quality of Jorge Guillén's poetry, enthusiastic
affirmation. In *Cántico* he declares that this is his natural predisposition: *"¡Afirmación, que es hambre: mi instinto siempre
diestro!"* (p. 238). One would do him injustice, however, were

39

one to assume that this affirmation is always given to him easily and naïvely. Here, as in so many other aspects of his poetry, enter the firm decision, the effort, the desire to discover the positive aspects. *Cántico* was followed by *Clamor,* a necessary complement that testifies to the full consciousness of the poet. There satire and elegy are given an important place. In *Homenaje* the affirmative tone is also interrupted at times. One can find there lines like the following: *"Hiede el mundo a su agonía"* (p. 61). They are not numerous, however. If distance is created between the one who contemplates and the object contemplated, this is done not with an ironic intention, but rather in order to affirm:

> El vivir es también comedia, por fortuna.
> Así se le soporta, mejor se le domina.
>> —*H,* 20

The ultimate hope never disappears. Suffice it to observe that desire in the evolution of one theme, Spain. In *Clamor* a certain bitterness was noticeable; the greater part of poems dealing with the poet's present circumstance, apart from the nostalgic ones, showed a rather negative tone. In *Homenaje* without trying to embellish the existing situation, the poet speaks of hope again, hope in the future:

> Hubo ardor. ¿Hoy cenizas? Una brasa.
> Arde bien. Arde siempre.
>> —*H,* 89

Jorge Guillén affirms constantly his ties with reality: a reality that he observes, like Galdós, but also a reality that achieves completion by re-creation: *"A la realidad ya toca / Con su potencia el lenguaje"* (*H,* 151). In *Cántico* he declares that reality always is greater than any dream or expectation. All of *Clamor* is recognition of this naked reality and shows a desire to distinguish in it bright tones that shine even against a gray background. Even when he, to use his own words, "vomits and rejects," he never loses his faith as a poet. In *Homenaje* he underlines again the importance of being able to dream with open eyes. Concrete presence is always a must in his amorous poems:

> Tú, mi clara
> Realidad, tú, tú dame
> La mano. Tú me salvas.
> —*H*, 252

When the question of the pure and the abstract arises, he gives the following advice, *"Procura / No tener siempre razón,"* exclaiming, *"¡Oh vida verdadera, vida impura!"* (p. 525). Stark reality is always accepted as the greatest value, as the most secure way to creativity. In a similar way if sometimes he has to face doubts or hesitations, these are also conquered with a very simple resolution, *"Sé tú mismo."* After an anguished interlude, peace is even more appreciated, and the poet pays tribute to the factor that has intervened in the reestablishment of order: *"¡Realidad! Y respiré"* (*H*, 534).

By affirming reality, he affirms the value of life itself. His aim is to live fully the life to which he has been destined and, with it, to create poetry. His homage to Juan Ruiz is most sincere in underlining that he was man above all. Even when he criticized he did so because of a joyous impulse. Guillén does not admit the possibility of being defeated, either. He never insinuates the possibility of breaking the ties with reality. Even that which seems negative always has a positive aspect:

"*¿Perra | Vida? Con amor*" (*H*, 28). In *Homenaje* as in the preceding works, he persists in paying the least possible attention to the theme of death. He does not try to escape it; he knows that the ultimate transition will have to be made once, but he does not wish this truth to prevent him from enjoying life while he can. In an admirable manner he finds a way of confronting it; he decides to consider old age as a mask, although he feels that at times this mask is claiming its own being. Only a man with enormous faith and hope is capable of doing this; only an ever growing thirst for life makes such hope possible:

> Feroz, feroz la vida,
> Tras su esperanza siempre.
> —*M*, 166

These were words from *Maremágnum*. In *Homenaje* while he observes this "*maremágnum*"—the entire world—he feels his heart rebel against sorrow caused by death, and he discovers an affirmative side even in this phenomenon: "*¿Tanta muerte no pare sin cesar esperanza?*" (p. 185). Now he can look at his own old age from a joyous perspective:

> Sé ahora de mi edad por el dorado
> Rayo que en esta tarde me ilumina
> Mi fuerza de fervor, mi afán maduro.
>
> Un benévolo duende está a mi lado.
> Es ya bella en la rosa hasta la espina.
> Contra la edad se alza mi futuro.
> —*M*, 299

The will power in confirming the unity of his total works brings back to *Homenaje* the main themes of *Cántico:* the light of the dawn produces the same ecstasy; the awakening is again sensed as a privileged state because it permits the return to full consciousness. It now acquires one more aspect: asking himself how the others ought to address him, the poet arrives at the joyous conclusion that in the mornings he can be greeted with a simple "Jorge," without adding the respectful *"don."* This is the hour in which he is full of vigor and enthusiasm. All in the morning tends to confirm him:

> Despertar.
>   Y la mano ya se tiende
> Para en seguida poseer un trozo
> De inmenso mundo, superior—no hay duda—
> A esa mano pequeña, muy pequeña,
> Al borde nada más de un infinito.
>
> —*H*, 522

Noon also is glorified in this book; the mature and serene gaiety of the hour of plenitude is evident. *Homenaje* also has hours in which it seems that *"todo en el aire es pájaro,"* and it continues to exalt the *"redondo Ahora"* of *Cántico*. The poet continues to ask whether today is not more valuable than tomorrow: *"Bien abrazado, el presente es quien entrega más tiempo intenso. ¡Ahora!"* (p. 485). The categorical affirmation that the greatest joy is *"ser, nada más"* is repeated with similar conciseness:

> Todos, seres. Y son: suprema
> Certidumbre. Basta a un destino.
> El poeta puede ser noble.
>
> —*H*, 139

The first poem of *Homenaje* is dedicated to the song; the

second praises beauty. The desire for beauty as substance and form is equally strong; it is necessary in order to be able to sing his song of praise:

> La vil palabra, no. Se opone al canto
> Mínimo del amor que bien se cumple.
> —*H,* 44

The affirmation of the universe would be incomplete if a special praise were not dedicated to the woman, always "the" woman, the only one who responds to *"Tú."* The central part of *Homenaje* consists of a long love poem, so vivid, so full of tenderness that even in its maturity it has a juvenile tone. Only through this amorous contact, always urgent, can plenitude of vital experience be achieved. Through love the here and now acquires new meaning and makes possible perfect creation.

Homenaje finds a solution to maintaining the continuity of the poet's attitude toward time, so different in the two preceding books: ahistoric in *Cántico, "Tiempo de Historia"* in *Clamor.* Now the two are united. In the amorous poems history remains "behind closed doors," imminent, but not disturbing. On the other hand, when the poet contemplates exterior beauty—*Retorno a Florencia*—he sees positive value in it: history adds

> un no sé qué de ambiente
> Más sutil y elegante que el presente
> Sólo actual de la hora sólo mía.
> —*H,* 557

The same positive aspect is seen when considering life as history: the years, the actions guided by the same firm decision accumulate joys and successes that complement the present jubilant hour.

Joy and exultation are familiar to the reader of *Cántico* who recalls that their most sublime form is happiness that can be shared. In solitude it is necessarily limited; it does not have perspective. Only communion leads to plenitude. The contact that always enriches must be seen with gratefulness:

> Gracias, profundamente gracias,
> Criatura de mediación.
> Mi vida trasciende contigo
> Sus límites.
>
> —*H*, 279

The necessity of sharing joys and sorrows makes life in common imperative: a difficult, but not undesirable task. In *Cántico* as well as in *Clamor* "the masses" appear as a negative factor. Real comprehension is possible only in personal—and limited—contact. The final result that man should be striving for, a perfectly harmonious chord, makes the effort worth while. A poem in *Homenaje, Del contacto al acto,* expounds the entire process:

> ¡Ah, la sociedad!
> Nunca estará bien hecho el mundo humano.
> Humanas criaturas hay capaces
> De residir en esencial acorde. . . .
>
> No se fracasa por deber diario.
> Vivir no es cultivar una impotencia.
> Varón será quien ame poseyendo.
> —¿Acorde?—Poderío suficiente
> Para asir esta vida. . . .
>
> —*H*, 494

Homenaje consists partly of this desire to understand and to share made reality. In the motto of *Variaciones* the poet suggests that the greatest delight is to understand a friend; the entire section represents a re-living and re-creating of the work of poets considered friends.

The attention that the poet gives to the works of others reveals in him the quality of a perfect reader, a reader whom he would like to find for his own works. In *Cántico* he declares that for him writing is not exercise leading to perfection, that his immediate aim is contact with the reader. *Homenaje* confirms this attitude and, as it has done with other aspects, clarifies it. The poet says that he does not address himself to the immense majority nor to the immense minority, but rather *"al hombre con toda su hombría."* He writes for a man who is capable of understanding him and feeling his experiences, for a reader willing to co-operate in the act of creation:

> Claro desfile de versos
> Que sin romper el negror
> De la noche a mí me alumbran.
> Se funden cadencia y luz:
> Palabra hacia poesía.
> Que se cumple acaso en ti,
> En tu instante de poeta,
> > Mi lector.
> > > —*H,* 517

The circle is now complete: inspired by the universe and the man who lives in it, by means of his sensitivity as man and his mastery as poet, the author has produced his work and is offering it to the reader who, like him, is a man. In this process he has accomplished the "perfect mystery" that he had sensed in the perfection of the circle; in it he remains, even in *Homenaje* aspiring to this perfection.

This brief summary of Guillén's vital themes and attitudes aspires chiefly to show that the work as we read and admire it has been possible thanks to a firm, clear will. The poet who from the beginning considered himself *"por vocación dispuesto / Siempre a la maravilla"* (*Q,* 148) crossed his life in search of it. In *Homenaje* he completes the preceding declaration: *"El arte de vivir ya vence al hado"* (p. 133). The predisposition alone would not have been sufficient; it only serves as an introduction. The rest has been a constant and conscious affirmation: the will to live and to enjoy the experience, to create affirming himself. All that appeared in suspense, vaguely foreseen, has been realized; the truth assumed in his verse has become living truth.

Going back to the line that has motivated these considerations, *"una gloria ya madura bajo mi firme decisión,"* one does not encounter difficulty in justifying the use of the adjective "mature." What we sense in *Homenaje* is precisely this, a mature glory. The firm decision appears dynamic, vibrant, full of juvenile impulse in *Cántico*. The interrupted lines, the exclamations, and the frequent irregularity of rhythm transmit the enthusiasm of youth. In *Homenaje* maturity makes the verse flow more regularly and calmly; often a whole poem emerges from a single, ample movement. Exclamations have become less frequent; one senses less impatience. The will that one encounters here is more serene and peaceful:

> Heme aquí. Desperté. Me ciñe el mundo
> Con el sosiego amable que le impongo.
>
> —*H,* 553

47

It is the serenity earned by the *"jornalero real,"* in which affirmative values continue to shine: *"El crepúsculo es noble si es sereno"* (*H*, 53). The whole life of the poet has been a constant maturing, a constant clarification with the help of poetry. Now, considering what has been achieved, the poet may well put on an equal level the three activities among which it has been divided: to be, to live, to create:

> Mi ser es mi vivir acumulado. . . .
> El de veras humilde pone el peso
> De su ser en su hacer: yo soy mi suma.
> De pretensión a realidad regreso.
> —*H*, 594[6]

[6] See also Biruté Ciplijauskaité, "The Joy in Jorge Guillén," *Books Abroad*, Vol. XLII, No. 1 (Winter, 1968), 28–32.

Humanism and Actuality in Jorge Guillén

by PIERRE DARMANGEAT

To SPEAK OF A POET is always to speak of oneself, however objective one may attempt to be. Perhaps it is more worthwhile for the reader to say simply what he owes to the poet.

First, the delight of the mind. This exacting style, which appears difficult because it is economical with words on which it confers an uncommon breadth, a multiple brilliance. The language is that of everyday, only more concentrated, dense, and muscular, the supreme source of its power. The first and most obvious virtue of Guillén's poetry is that it rewards attentive reading, a quality essential in a time when everything conspires to deprive man of his most precious faculty of attentiveness.

Guillén asks the co-operation of his reader. He respects him and wishes him the best in the world:

Para el hombre es la hermosura.

Thus is rehabilitated, outside the ivory tower and without any vain romanticism, alive and in our midst, the beauty that some have wished (and still wish, occasionally) to deny in the name of man. Beauty is on all sides for us to see. In Guillén the capacity to be amazed by the sights of the everyday world remains as fresh at seventy-five as it was at twenty-five. Fools will say that he is astonished at nothing. Fools neither see nor hear. The poet *"donne à voir,"* according to Éluard's fine formula. Guillén marvels at the fresh beginning, at the infinitely various continuation of all things. Each morning, each hour of the day is a unique work of art.

Far from getting lost in a cold aestheticism, love of beauty reveals the beauty of love. Never has carnal love inspired verses more deserving of their object. *Salvación de la primavera* is the canticle of love-play, glorious, jubilant, serious, without the shadows of false shame and still less of ostentation. Here modern lyricism regains the vital impulse, the freedom of the ancients, but it combines with it, in tenderness and the gift of self, a quality of soul which was to them unknown.

Nothing is to be inevitably deduced in a man's development. But why be surprised that the man who is probably the most intelligent poet of his generation, should also be one of the most sensitive, and that he who has sung so well the love of a man and a woman, then the love of the father and that of the grandfather, should respond to the shock of events with all his being?

By attempting to enclose the poet of *Cántico* within a narrow aesthetic that is foreign to him,[1] a number of people prepared for themselves the surprise, agreeable or not, according to taste, of *Clamor*. They did not see what the evidence was, however: that *Clamor* is already promised in *Cántico,* which is continued in various degrees into the pages of *Maremágnum,* ... *Que van a dar en la mar,* and *A la altura de las circunstancias.*

---

[1] I do not repeat here what I have written on the so-called *"poésie pure"* and on the Valéry-Guillén relations in *Jorge Guillén ou le Cantique émerveillé,* (Paris, Librairie des Editions Espagnoles, 1958).

Ivar Ivask, left, with Jorge Guillén, University of Oklahoma,
February 10, 1968.

Photo Credit: Tom Blevins (*The Norman Transcript*)

A hasty perusal suffices to show that *Cara a cara,* or *A pesar de todo,* to cite only two titles, announce certain flashes, and flash forth themselves in accents very different from *Niño* or *El aire;* and that *Tréboles* or *Lugar de Lázaro,* each in its way, is a variation on themes dear to the author of *Cántico.*[2]

Fidelity to oneself is not inflexibility. Guillén's poetry, at first the sensitive and radiant object of a happy time (the first *Cántico,* 1928), becomes with the thread of the years an intimate journal, a mirror, a clear and courageous witness to the history which turned upside down, first Spain, then the entire civilized world, without in any sense renouncing the deep-voiced song, the fundamental canticle:

A ningún fervor yo renuncio . . .

These values, in no way contradictory, but rather complementary, assume faith in man. What else could be expressed in poems so different in appearance as *Tentaciones de Antonio* and *Como tú, lector?* One sees from these examples that humanity, far from being given to Guillén, is an end to be attained. Better yet, the being that he will never finish making, disengaging himself from personal or exterior temptations, from false ideologies, from hostile forces. Guillén's humanism looks forward, like that of the true classics. Thus, the man of the year 2000 will be able to recognize himself, according to this present one, in his *"señorío de piel."*

I do not think that there is in the poetry of our time anything more important than Guillén's two great books, while we await *Homenaje,* which is no doubt near. In reading and re-

[2] I have explained this point in *De Cántico a Clamor ou la continuité d'un poète,* in *Mélanges à la mémoire de Jean Sarrailh,* Vol. I (Paris, Centre de Recherches de l'Institut d'Etudes Hispaniques, 1966).

reading this poet, one feels oneself becoming more intelligent, better, and more nobly and more authentically humane. One does better than admire him: one loves him.

Translated from the French by CONSTANCE WAGNER

Cántico, Clamor, and Homenaje: The Concrete and the Universal

by Andrew P. Debicki

Jorge Guillén's poetry has often been treated as if it were composed of two different kinds of works. *Cántico,* which contains the poet's earlier verse, has most often been evaluated as "pure poetry," as the foremost example of the supposedly abstract orientation of the Spanish "Generation of the 1920's"; the three volumes of *Clamor,* which contain later poems, have been deemed "social poetry," concerned with the immediate realities of our modern world.[1] Such views of Guillén's poetry have even led José María Castellet to argue that the poet, after an epoch of inhuman formalism, "recants" under the impact of historical circumstances and becomes more "human" in his writing. Guillén's supposed recantation is used by Castellet to

---

[1] *Cántico* has appeared in five editions, dated 1928, 1936, 1945, 1950, and 1962; new poems are included in the second, third, and fourth editions. All quotations in this article are taken from the fourth edition. *Clamor: Tiempo de historia* consists of three volumes, *Maremágnum,* 1957; . . . *Que van a dar en la mar,* 1960; and *A la altura de las circunstancias,* 1963.

For a discussion of the "purity" of *Cántico* and the "humanity" of *Clamor,* see José María Castellet, *Veinte años de poesía española (1939–1959),* 3rd edition (Barcelona, Ed. Seix Barral, 1962), 92. See also Luis Cernuda, *Estudios sobre poesía española contemporánea* (Madrid, Ed. Guadarrama, 1957), 187–89, 193. A much more balanced, and to my mind accurate, view of *Cántico*'s "purity" is offered by Joaquín Casalduero in *Cántico de Jorge Guillén* (Madrid, Ed. Victoriano Suárez, 1953), 35–57, 98–99, 201–202; and by Ricardo Gullón and José María Blecua in *La poesía de Jorge Guillén* (Zaragoza, *Heraldo de Aragón,* 1949).

support his whole view of the "Generation of the 1920's" as a group of purists who have had to "repent" and change their outlook.[2]

Such a view, in my opinion, does a disservice to Guillén's poetry by ignoring its fundamental unity and some of its basic traits. Elsewhere I have studied different ways in which the poems of *Cántico* combine a sense of physical immediacy with visions of more absolute implications.[3] It seems to me, in fact, that such a combination of the concrete and the absolute is a dominant note of all of Guillén's poetry. It enables Guillén to take into account both the particulars of our existence and the essential themes and problems which underlie this existence. In different ways and with differing emphases, all three major poetic books of Guillén—*Cántico, Clamor,* and *Homenaje*— achieve this successful fusion of the specific and the absolute.

In *Cántico* this fusion is most frequently achieved through the use of nature images. Natural elements are personified, for example, to lead the reader simultaneously toward both a specific concrete experience and an essential theme. We can see this at the beginning of *Los nombres:*

> Albor. El horizonte
> Entreabre sus pestañas
> Y empieza a ver. ¿Qué? Nombres.
> Están sobre la pátina
>
> De las cosas.
>
> —*C, 26*

[2] See Castellet, pp. 43–48 and 89–100.

[3] See my "Jorge Guillén's *Cántico*," *PMLA, Vol. LXXXI* (1966), 439–45. A somewhat different view of the relationship between the concrete and the abstract in *Cántico* is presented by Dámaso Alonso in *Poetas españoles contemporáneos* (Madrid, Ed. Gredos, 1952), 235–43.

The poem begins by personifying the horizon: the semicircle of dawn light which pushes back the darkness is identified with an opening eye which pushes back its eyelid. The detailed visual parallel forces us to notice a natural phenomenon often taken for granted and to link it with an action of our own. In this way the image gives sensorial immediacy to a natural element. At the same time, by attributing the power of sight to the horizon, it transforms and conceptualizes the scene, and it leads us to a very abstract theme: the need to seize the essences (names) of the fleeting realities of our world. On examining our reactions to this image, we can see that the two diverse reactions, the sensorial and the abstract, which it evokes in us, are produced by the same words. These reactions are simultaneous and intertwined. The effect of this image is later duplicated by the whole poem, which conveys both the excitement of tangible reality and the need to see this reality through its names, those essences which make it timeless.[4]

A very similar effect is created in *Impaciente vivir:*

Salta por el asfalto,
Frente al anochecer,
El ventarrón de marzo,
Tan duro que se ve.

Las esquinas aguzan
Su coraje incisivo.
Tiemblan desgarraduras
De viento y sol. ¿Gemidos?

Una lid: cuatro calles.
La luz bamboleada,

[4] For an excellent thematic study of this poem, see Concha Zardoya, *Poesía española contemporánea* (Madrid, Ed. Guadarrama, 1961), 298.

Luz apenas, retrae
Las figuras a manchas.

Da el viento anochecido
Contra esquina y sillar.
Marzo arrecia. ¿Granito?
El lo acometerá.

Entonces, por la piedra
Rebotando, se yergue
Con mas gana la fuerza
Del vivir impaciente.

—C, 46

In turning the meeting of wind and city into a battle between live beings, the poem makes the confrontation tangible.
By making the wind jump, by describing its hardness as visible,
and by pinpointing the episode in place and time (*"asfalto,"*
"anochecer," "marzo"), the poem gives sensory immediacy to
an event we might otherwise dismiss as trivial. Likewise, the
personification of corners as warriors makes us experience concretely the normally insignificant hardness of common objects. By defining the noise of the wind as a moan, by making
the light an active participant in stanza four, and by further
personifying the wind in stanza five (using the adjective *"anochecido"* instead of saying *"del anochecer"*)—in all these ways
Guillén gives tangibility to a common event.

The very same images and personifications however, also
serve to carry us beyond the particulars of the scene. The attri-
bution of an abstract human trait (*"coraje"*) to the wind and
the implication that this wind makes a considered choice in
attacking (*"¿Granito? El lo acometerá"*) takes it out of the
realm of ordinary nature. Transformed into an image of pur-

poseful activity, it comes to stand for more than itself, to represent a general force of life. By so personifying a common storm, Guillén calls attention to this poem as an elaborate poetic construct and to the wind as a deliberate symbol for something more important than a chance shift in weather.

In the final stanza the theme of the poem becomes explicit: the wind and the whole scene convey to the speaker a sense of the force of life. We accept this view held by the speaker. We do so because the personifications and images used in the poem have transmitted to us, simultaneously, both the reality of the scene and its role as a symbol. We have been made to apprehend the wind both as a vivid particular experience and as an artful representation of a wider pattern. We have come to feel the immediacy of a specific scene and, at the same time, to see an ample scheme of life. *"Impaciente vivir"* has become for us a full embodiment of an experience at once vital and absolute.

The two examples of personifications which we have just seen appear in poems dealing with basic philosophic themes: the essences of objects and the force of life. In other poems of *Cántico* (*Las llamas* and *Los balcones del oriente*) similar personifications are used in connection with other such themes: the search for absolutes and the triviality of an everyday existence. In each case the technique used, by simultaneously pointing to such a wider theme and giving immediacy to the scene described, takes the theme out of the realm of abstract philosophy and immerses it in our world, a world in which mental and physical realities are intertwined, in which absolute questions come to us through concrete experiences. Guillén has used personifications as organizing principles which fuse the specific and the absolute levels of his poems into single, cohesive realities and which make the meanings conveyed by his poems at once concrete

57

and fundamental. He has achieved, as a result, that unity in complexity which William Wimsatt deems the attribute of a valuable poem, a "concrete universal."[5]

A similar fusion of the particular and the absolute is achieved in other poems of *Cántico* by somewhat diverse means. The ending of *Perfección* furnishes an example:

> Y tanto se da el presente
> Que el pie caminante siente
> La integridad del planeta.
> —*C*, 240

The image used focuses on a physical contact between the protagonist and the ground, calling attention to the concrete scene; yet the same image also points to the wider issue of Man's feeling of harmony with the world. In like fashion Guillén uses a tangible link between the protagonist and a natural element in *Además* (p. 127) and *Quiero dormir* (p. 436) both to give reality to a particular scene and to point to a wider issue.

In *Muerte a lo lejos* Guillén links the concrete and the absolute by presenting a conceptual theme through nature images:

> Alguna vez me angustia una certeza,
> Y ante mí se estremece mi futuro.
> Acechándole está de pronto un muro
> Del arrabal final en que tropieza
>
> La luz del campo. ¿Más habrá tristeza
> Si la desnuda el sol? No, no hay apuro

[5] See Wimsatt, "The Concrete Universal," *The Verbal Icon*, 2nd edition, (New York, Noonday Press, 1958), 69–83.

Todavía. Lo urgente es el maduro
Fruto. La mano ya le descorteza.

. . . Y un día entre los días el más triste
Será. Tenderse deberá la mano
Sin afán. Y acatando el inminente

Poder diré sin lágrimas: embiste
Justa fatalidad. El muro cano
Va a imponerme su ley, no su accidente.
      —*C,* 281

The first stanza stresses the horrors of dying, but the poem
then shifts dramatically in tone and reveals a calm acceptance of
death. The image of the light obstructed by the wall and put
out by the sunset makes death more tangible, more a part of
immediate existence; it avoids any hollow rhetoric or any grandiose overstatement. But this same image also links death to a
perennial cyclic process of nature, and in that way transfers
it from the realm of the personal to that of universal patterns.
The image thus simultaneously relates the issue of death to the
most immediate and most absolute points of view. In both ways
it justifies the outlook of the poem: because death is both a
common happening and a part of the pattern of existence, it
is not an enigma to be feared but a happening to be accepted
in the course of things.

 Guillén reinforces this view by making life a concrete but
symbolic fruit, naturally developing and naturally being
stripped away. He also accents the naturalness of death by shift-
ing to a colloquial language in the second and third stanzas
and by creating a matter-of-fact tone through run-on lines combined with abrupt breaks in the middle of each. The reader,

after the flowing hendecasyllable of the somewhat grandiose first stanza, is brought back to a calm and direct outlook. These techniques support the natural images in making us envision death as a very common and immediate, yet also very fundamental, truth to be accepted.

All the techniques and poems which we have observed make evident, to my mind, Guillén's success in fusing and conveying a concrete experience and an absolute theme simultaneously. The poems encompass different facets of human existence: happenings such as the coming of dawn, a gale in the city, and the birth of a child and themes such as the force of life, the problem of death, the order of the universe, and the value of life in the face of time. The book in no way shows an escape from particular human problems. It does, it is true, avoid presenting these problems for descriptive or social purposes; it always connects them, instead, to larger questions, to basic themes. Based on events which could have seemed fleetingly insignificant and leading to themes which could have been treated abstractly, *Cántico* again and again links these diverse elements into a single and cohesive whole, immediate and significant at the same time. It offers us, thanks to its poetic art, a series of "concrete universals."

Throughout the three volumes of *Clamor,* we find frequent allusions to the common objects of our daily lives, to ordinary happenings of the contemporary world. We also find a more frequent use of ordinary, prosaic language as well as of anecdote. All this seems to suggest that Guillén's poetry is evolving to realism and even to "social literature." To my mind, however, there is no such evolution; the everyday elements present in the book are used for a very different end.

One should note at the outset that wider themes are in no

way absent from *Clamor*. If *Maremágnum,* the first volume, focuses on the sufferings of man in our time, . . . *Que van a dar en la mar,* the second, stresses the terrors of time and death in conflict with the positive forces of life and love. *A la altura de las circunstancias,* the third volume, picks up the fears and anxieties present in the earlier two; in the face of them it portrays Man's struggle to assert his dignity and his value. Man's striving to avoid the double dangers of bestiality and of inhuman abstraction and thus overcome the temptations of our world is a key theme of this book, as Miss Ciplijauskaité has already pointed out in an excellent article.[6] In this *A la altura* parallels *Cántico;* whereas *Cántico* asserts a general delight in the force of life, *A la altura* underlines the value of existence in the circumstances of our times. The title itself makes this clear.

The specific episodes and happenings present in *Clamor* are closely related to the wider themes of the book. Much as he did in *Cántico,* Guillén always fuses inextricably the particular and the absolute levels of his poems, producing works at the same time concrete and universal. This time, however, he uses somewhat different ingredients and techniques to engender the fusion. This is especially apparent in *A la altura de las circunstancias.*

Quite frequently the link between a particular reality and a wider theme is established by a common object:

> Un bichito surca esa miel,
> Enorme—como Vía Láctea
> Para mí, más incierto que él.
> —*A la altura,* 81

[6] See Biruté Ciplijauskaité, *"Clamor a la altura de las circunstancias,"* *Revista Hispánica Moderna,* Vol. XXIX, (1963), 290–93; see also sections II and IV of *A la altura,* which portray the quests of Sancho Panza and Saint Anthony for a human outlook, one neither animalistic nor entirely abstract.

El calor abre las ventanas:
Cuartos en su luz encendida.
Más estrellas menos lejanas.
                    —*Ibid.,* 91

In each of these short *tréboles,* Guillén describes a very common scene—a bug in honey or open windows on a hot summer night. In each he also makes his description point to larger themes—Man's uncertainty in the universe or the presence of ideals in our daily world. In each poem the link between these two levels is produced largely by a visual resemblance: a bug swimming in honey seems to imitate a man moving in space, suggesting Man's search for orientation; a window seen from far off resembles a star, thus suggesting ideals. Such visual correspondences make us accept the link between the ordinary realities and the abstract themes presented in these poems. Somewhat like the personifications and the natural images seen in *Cántico,* the objects described here make us receive together and connect an immediate reality and a wider issue.

It is worth noting that in the first of these two short poems Guillén uses an insignificant object and a trivial daily happening. It is also worth observing that this poem contains a note of irony. By comparing himself with the bug, the poem's protagonist understates his anguish and mocks himself, rather than making his suffering seem grandiose. This does not negate the seriousness of his predicament; man's pettiness and his impotence in the face of the universe are, if anything, increased by the image. But it does avoid the danger that the protagonist might seem egotistic or rhetorical to us, or that his situation might seem overblown. Thanks to the irony, the protagonist emerges instead as a man who can recognize his predicament and his limitations, who can see himself in a wider perspective.

A similar irony appears in another *trébol:*

Gran poeta: gran calamar
Que por el agua arroja tinta
Soñando con ser todo el mar.
       —A la altura, 81

This image is again based on a concrete parallel between a squid
and a poet who writes furiously. Guillén takes advantage of a
visual resemblance and of a double meaning in linking the
idiom *"derramar tinta"* (to write rapidly) with the physical
action of the squid. The connection between squid and poet, of
course, produces irony and mocks the man. In this fashion it
makes us see that the speaker is able to laugh at himself and his
activities, that he has a sense of his shortcomings and is in no
way haughty or remote. We still see this speaker, of course, as
a being desperately trying to assert his vision; we even sympa-
thize more with him because of his awareness of his limitations.
Guillén, using irony somewhat in the way described by Robert
Penn Warren in "Pure and Impure Poetry," has avoided any
remote grandiloquence, has expressed a significant human
plight, the desire to construct an important work in a down-
to-earth way.[7]

The irony and the use of prosaic objects and scenes differentiate these poems of *Clamor* from the ones of *Cántico* on
which I have commented. These techniques accent the shortcomings of the world and the protagonist. They make the immediate reality described fuller of the trivial and the grotesque, and

---

[7] See Warren, "Pure and Impure Poetry," published in the *Kenyon Review,*
Spring, 1943, and reprinted in *Criticism: The Foundations of Modern Literary
Judgment,* ed. by Mark Schorer (New York, Harcourt, Brace & Co., 1948), 367–
78. It might be useful to note that irony is employed in many other poems of
Clamor, such as pp. 92 and 103 of *A la altura,* and pp. 100 and 176 of *Mare-
mágnum.*

they make the protagonist more aware of the limitations both in and around him. But they in no way destroy the link between the immediate events and the absolute themes; indeed, they enhance it. They identify the speakers as limited human beings like us, living in our common world, nevertheless seeking (and finding) wider concerns and wider visions around them.

This is even more apparent in *El primer té*:

> La mañana se abre camino
> Por entre luces dentro y fuera
> De unas mansiones sumergidas
> En niebla-sueño y sueño-niebla.
> Cala un frío con soledad
> Que sería injusta. . . . No. Llega
> Suave salvación por silencio
> De servicio. Ya está. Bandeja.
> Dice el durmiente despertándose:
> Gracias. (Sabiduría inglesa.)
> —*A la altura,* 75

The poem does not seem at first to have a very far-reaching theme. The first six lines present two conflicting attitudes on the part of a man who is waking up in the morning. In the first four lines the man is in a state of peaceful lethargy—a lethargy emphasized by the images of revery and by the use of one long phrase. Suddenly the tone is broken in line five; the verb *"cala,"* the cold and the solitude, the two abrupt breaks, and the "no" of line six all create a harsh mood. The man's contentment has suddenly been destroyed.

The rest of the poem suggests a return to calm and order. The solution is represented by a servant who brings an early breakfast to the protagonist. The run-on verse between lines six and seven, the alliteration in *"s,"* and the idea of a "soft

salvation" all point to a renewed peace. Yet we remain somewhat apprehensive. It is difficult to accept the unexciting arrival
of breakfast as a satisfactory solution to the protagonist's jar-
ring loneliness. The expression *"de servicio"* and the allusion
to a tray underline the prosaic, intranscendent nature of the
event. Yet, taking the whole situation into account, the arrival
of the breakfast (the British early morning tea) can be read
as an ordinary act which, nevertheless, does establish contact
between human beings, eliminates the momentary loneliness of
the protagonist, and permits him to function normally and po-
litely in the world. The contrast between the commonplace expressions of line eight and the smooth image of line seven defines the double aspect of the episode: it is insignificant in itself,
and yet it has great value for the lonely guest who thankfully
accepts it.

The ambiguity which we have sensed in this poem has a
definite purpose. It makes us feel the dual nature of the early
morning tea: an activity insignificant and dull on the one hand,
yet meaningful as a way of helping a man break out of his loneliness on the other. This in turn suggests a wider theme: the
possibility of finding amidst the most common of acts
significant values and experiences. This theme in turn connects
with a major issue treated by the volume: the finding of important values in the everyday modern world.

We can see irony in *El primer té,* just as we did in the
poems previously discussed. By making breakfast a "salvation,"
Guillén links the petty with the sublime. This irony may point
out the shortcomings of modern life, but above all it reinforces
the poem's theme, making us feel that we can miraculously
find wider values even in the most trivial of happenings. It
serves, then, to underline the link between our immediate circumstances and absolute issues.

In the poem *Cita* (*A la altura,* pp. 34–38), Guillén has a protagonist cross a city full of traffic in order to meet his loved one. The situation is mocked by juxtaposing the petty aspects of a modern city—traffic, soap advertisements, nameless crowds—to mythical allusions and to poetic images. This mocks modern life, of course. It finally leads not to social criticism but to a view of the modern city as a place in which essential themes and issues are lowered. The meeting to which the protagonist is hurrying emerges as a microcosm of a romantic lovers' tryst. And the whole poem makes us feel that in our world there can be found ample issues, though diminished by the plain nature of our surroundings. *Cita* combines the use of contemporary allusions, of irony, and of anecdote to establish again a relationship between the immediate and the far-reaching.

In all these poems of *A la altura de las circunstancias,* Guillén has linked particular elements with wider issues. In now using common events, images, irony, and anecdote, he undoubtedly places greater stress on the shortcomings of our modern world; but he also points up, through these techniques, the absolute themes which are present in this world and which can emerge from our concrete existence.[8] Avoiding both the mere presentation of ethereally abstract themes and the simple concern with the specifics of our world, Guillén offers us again a series of "concrete universals."

On first impression *Homenaje* resembles *Cántico* more than it does *Clamor.* The work frequently focuses on a place, a natural image, or a literary allusion, and simultaneously evokes

---

[8] It should be noted that *A la altura* contains poems which embody essential themes through natural images in a manner similar to that seen in *Cántico.* See for example pp. 20, 78, 93, 95, and 107.

One of the display cases of the Jorge Guillén Exhibit held in the Bizzell Memorial Library concurrently with the conference in February, 1968.

a wider philosophic theme. It does not contain many descriptions of common objects, many examples of prosaic expressions, or many allusions to everyday events. It is generally free of the irony so dominant in *Clamor*.

Yet the book shares traits which we first saw in *Clamor*. It contains many poems based on specific anecdotes: visits to given places, happenings in literary works read, several love episodes. It alludes to a variety of specific locations, literary works, and authors. It seems to contain autobiographical material, always transformed and used for wider poetic purposes. (In *Lo personal,* on p. 510 of *Homenaje,* Guillén points out how the biography portrayed transcends himself. It is the autobiography *"del hombre, ya no mía."*) The poems of *Homenaje* seem to base themselves more explicitly on the materials of our world, our lives, and our literary traditions than did those of *Cántico,* while at the same time minimizing the attention given to the ordinary features of the contemporary scene which were evident in *Clamor*. Guillén seems to leave behind his concern for a specific prosaic society but continues to find in particular human events and experiences the sources of his art.

Homenaje contains many more references to poetry and to art than Guillén's earlier books. The volume, dedicated *"A todas las musas,"* contains many poems paying homage to other works and writers; it comprises many other poems which allude to literary places and events; and it frequently refers to the tasks, goals, and achievements of the poet and the artist. One theme appears again and again in *Homenaje:* the artist's power to evoke and preserve in time and from death the transitory meanings and experiences of men. This theme is handled directly in some poems like *Palacio* and *Superación*. It is implied frequently when Guillén evokes the vital meanings which so many poems of the past hold for us and when he addresses his own work to all readers of the future. (See p. 513 and the *Dedicatoria final*.)

We might say, then, that in *Homenaje* Guillén treats explicitly a feature of poetry which we have seen exemplified by his own verse: its way of connecting the immediate and the universal, of finding in the transitory the roots of the absolute. But *Homenaje* does not limit itself to talking about this view of poetry; it also embodies it. Some of its poems, it is true, seem dominated by a discussion of the poet's goals; many seem to stress the philosophic implications of the value of poetry. But we also find throughout the book works which exemplify a poetic linking of the concrete and the universal.

Guillén's exposition of the vitality and universality of great art is clear in *Superación*, which mentions and refutes the view that Jorge Manrique's work is dated and alien to the modern reader:

> Manrique va hasta el hombre en general:
> El que se muere. Tú también y yo,
> Y todos "los que viven por sus manos
> Y los ricos" de hoy, del siglo xv.
> A mí, lector del xx, me conturban
> Los sigilosos pasos de la muerte
> Que de puntillas anda "tan callando"
> Tras alguien, sabe Dios, ahora mismo.
> —*H, 502*

By picking up Manrique's own image of a personified death creeping up on Man, Guillén reminds us of both the concreteness and the wider impact of the *Coplas a la muerte de su padre*. In referring to Manrique's description of the laborers and the rich, Guillén points out that the fifteenth-century poet seized concretely an enduring scheme of human life. Guillén

68

focuses precisely on images which permit Manrique—just as
they permit Jorge Guillén—to present his vision both tangibly
and absolutely, and thus to remain accessible to readers of all
times. In the poem *Navidad en Piazza Navona* Guillén again
stresses the way in which key meanings are concretely em-
bodied in art:

> La Navidad: un Nacimiento
> Con sus figurillas de aldea,
> Más aldeana si es de barro.
> O sea. . . .
> Un dios sin forma no lo siento.
> Encarnarse debe la idea.
> Entiendo mejor lo que agarro.
> —*H*, 165

The Italian Nativity scene also presents Guillén's view of art as
a way of giving corporeal expression to absolute meanings.

If the poems we have just seen discuss the achievements
of the artist, *Palacio,* with the subtitle *Marina Adriática,* also
embodies them.

> El mármol blanco del palacio en losas
> De escalones desciende—valentía
> Firme que a un oleaje desafía—
> Hasta el agua y sus trazas tortuosas.
>
> Así, palacio, porque te desposas
> Con elemento siempre en móvil vía
> De roedor retorno y fuerza fría,
> Triunfas del mar, del tiempo y de sus fosas.
>
> Por ambición, por lujo, por capricho
> Más allá de los hábitos prudentes,
> Elevas la más frágil hermosura,

69

Nos dices lo que nadie nos ha dicho,
Desánimo a los hombres no consientes.
La más osada voluntad perdura.

—*H*, 158

The personification of the palace, like some of the ones in *Cántico,* produces two effects at once. By turning the palace's location at the shore into a descent, a challenge, and a combat, this personification changes a simple description into a vivid drama. It therefore prevents us from passing over the palace as a mere setting and makes us experience its particular location and attributes. The same personification also identifies the palace as a force battling against the destructive sea, as an artistic beauty asserting itself against the world and against time. The personification thus leads squarely to the wider theme of the work, the perduring qualities of the work of art.

A similar effect is produced by the personification of the water which not only becomes a specific element, cold and biting, but also suggests those destructive forces of time and the world against which the work of art must assert itself. This device, too, points to both the concrete and the absolute.

Guillén paradoxically makes the palace marry the water in stanza two, while he also has it defy the waves and overcome the sea. By doing so, he makes the work of art not only link itself to the world of nature which surrounds it but also stand out against it. He suggests that the work of art must draw on nature for its experience while also asserting its unique vision.

The personification of the palace is made more and more evident as the sonnet develops. In the first stanza it is only indicated by the actions of descending and challenging. In succeeding stanzas the palace is addressed directly, and in the last six verses it is praised as the embodiment of a human and

70

artistic struggle for perfection and permanence. This gradual intensification of the technique, and the consequent gradual elevation of the palace, lead us to a progressive change of emphasis as we read the poem. We begin by giving equal weight to the concrete level and to the wider implications of the battle of art against time. As the poem develops, and as the personification becomes more general and the visual imagery less noticeable, we give greater and greater stress to the latter. By the end of the work this more absolute level is dominant; it is supported by the conceptual and philosophical vocabulary of the last lines. This poem clearly leads us from the specific to the universal. This progression seems to differentiate *Palacio* from so many poems of *Cántico,* in which the concrete and the absolute levels remain fused throughout. And it suggests, perhaps, that in *Homenaje* Guillén places greater emphasis on the wider issues of poetry, just as he considers the role of the poet more directly and explicitly.

Throughout *Homenaje* Guillén frequently deals with the relationship between the poet's perception of the world around him and his creative use of language. In *Sospecha de foca,* subtitled *Maine,* he points out the collaboration taking place between the external world and the human viewer-poet.

El mar murmura grandeza.
¿Un punto negro en el agua?
Adivino la cabeza
De una foca. No la fragua
Mi magín, que nunca empieza.

Ondulación de oleaje
Sobre el dorso de una foca.
¿Encontré lo que yo traje?

A la realidad ya toca
Con su potencia el lenguaje.
                    —*H*, 151

Initially the seal is out there, independent of its observer. But once the latter starts describing it, what is given forth is a fusion of the seal's objective image and the viewpoint of its observer, who cannot determine the line of demarcation between the two (line 8). This observer-speaker fuses perception and creation in some undetermined combination; he seizes a particular reality and yet gives it perspective and expression.[9]

It is important to note how this poem is organized. Our attention is called, from the very beginning, to a specific and almost anecdotal scene: the coast of Maine and a particular speaker who is impressed by the sea's greatness and who suddenly spots a black dot which turns out to be a seal. In light of these details the speaker's initial awareness that the seal exists outside of his mind and his later realization that he is combining an external reality and a personal perspective seem to us perfectly acceptable as the normal meditations of a very specific, philosophically-inclined man in a certain situation. The description in lines 6 and 7 adds further to the particularity of the situation: we, like the speaker, can see individual waves sliding over the seal.

Yet the same point of view and the same details also direct us to the poem's larger theme. Characterizing the speaker as meditative and establishing him as a concrete being makes him someone apt to question the nature of poetic perception and creation. The statements in lines 4 and 5 not only give us

[9] The necessity of combining a perception of objects and a mastery of words, and of bringing the two together into a new entity, the poem, is also treated in *Candelabro* (*Homenaje*, p. 219).

the particular speaker's views about his experience but also stand as a general comment on how human and poetic perception is founded on reality. Even the description in lines 6 and 7, concrete as it is, makes us think about the wider question of perspectives. We wonder to what degree the waves' neat undulations over the back of the seal are a descriptive fact and to what degree they merely reflect the speaker's perspective. In this way we are led to wonder about the whole question of perception and creation and to duplicate the speaker's doubt of line 8. The same ingredients that make the poem concrete lead us to its absolute theme.

The last two lines of this poem, just like the ending of *Palacio,* clearly focus on the abstract level. We are made aware that the description of the seal by the speaker exemplifies the issue of poetic language and its connection to reality. We are left at the end with a perennial question about art: to what degree does it capture reality, to what degree does it create it?

If *Palacio* used "concrete universals" reminiscent of those in *Cántico*—personification and natural images—*Sospecha de foca* reveals techniques reminiscent of *Clamor*—a specific story and speaker. Yet both poems reveal a trait which appears principally in *Homenaje:* a shift to a directly philosophic presentation at the end. In this book as Guillén deals more explicitly with the nature of poetic art, as he not only creates but questions and defines poetry, he leads us more directly to the conceptual and absolute themes of his works.

We have seen how diverse poems of Jorge Guillén combine and convey at once the concrete particularity of their subjects and the more universal implications engendered by them. In *Cántico* this combination is often achieved by nature images, by elements of reality applicable to any place and any time. In *Clamor* this combination is created by anecdote, irony, and contemporary references, as Guillén finds his "concrete universals" in the elements of our particular contemporary setting. In *Homenaje* Guillén not only produces his concrete universals but also comments on them and presents more directly his views on poetic art. In somewhat diverse ways Guillén constantly offers us works which combine the vivid particulars and the absolutes, the immediate and the universal. Based on events which could have been fleetingly insignificant and on themes which could have become sterile abstractions, his works turn these materials, instead, into full and cohesive single realities, into good poems—poems which will, in their combined immediacy and universality, remain accessible to readers in centuries to come.

The Circle and Its Rupture in the Poetry of Jorge Guillén

by Eugenio Frutos

THE CIRCLE AND THE SPHERE are perfect figures in plane and tri-dimensional space respectively, according to the classical Greek conception. The cosmic process is cyclical—the eternal return of Heracles and Empedocles—and a solid sphere of equally divided mass is the image of the immutable being of Parmenides. Also, the stars were first thought of as discoid and later as spherical. Finally, human generations are compared in a well-known passage from Homer to the cyclical renewal of the leaves of the trees.

It does not seem strange then, in a poetry that probes the essential forms (although it is anchored in the concrete existence of the poet), that these geometrically-perfect forms should appear. But life is not only perfection, and when sorrow or the irrationality of the world intervenes, the pure forms are broken. I should like to show this aspect and this break in the poetry of Jorge Guillén with respect to the circle, although it could also be demonstrated with respect to the sphere.

The first *Cántico* (1928) is accepted in Guillén's poetry as representative of a poetry of the essential. The essential, however, may have always been included in the existential, since reality appears inherent in appearance, in the most immediate and evident appearances. It seems then that this "purity" would offer also the purest forms. And, in effect, "Perfection of the circle" appears thematically. But precisely in this poem the pure form, and at times the circle, appears least. This occurs because the mystery *"Invisible dentro/Del bloque del aire"* seems enclosed in a sphere. It is true that the circles do not correspond to spatial forms but to the perfection of the mystery: *"Misterio perfecto/Perfección del círculo, . . ."* The perfection consists in being a mystery without mystery, that is, a *"misterio sin sombra."*

Perhaps one should look for the purest part of the circle in its center, a point without extent, free of any tangible imperfection. I recall that *"Claridad/En un solo plano,"* from the poem *Tornasol,* in which *"esté presente/Como un firme sí/ Que responda siempre/Total, el confín."* Of course, a circular confine. Transposed to time, the center point of the circle will be the instant, or, rather, the *"redondo ahora,"* the *"absoluto Presente."* The center of the sphere is also a point: *"Cenit de una primavera/Redonda, perfecta esfera. . . ."* But when does this center open, widening into an abyss? I refer to the poem *Gran silencio:*

> Gran silencio. Se extiende a la redonda
> La infinitud de un absoluto raso.
> Una sima sin fin horada el centro.
> Y sin cesar girando, cae, cae
> Ya invisible y zumbón, celeste Círculo.

Before breaking through the borders, as in *Cántico,* the circle breaks in the center. But let us note the dynamism that moves and declines its motionless perfection and its impassivity. When the circle is not perfect, it is not a circle but "circular," as in abundant dynamism. Because *"Girando girando/Desaparecio/ Lo terso en lo raudo,"* so in the flight of the martins:

> Rondan los vencejos
> sin cesar ... ¡Oh cercos!

When the circle is plural, a vital impetus is multiplied. Thus, already in *Niña: "círculos de la rosa."* Or in *Meseta: "Horizontes en círculo/Se abren."* Or now in its vital concrete translation:

> y los aros de los niños
> Fatalmente multiplican
> Ondas de gracia sobrante,
> Para dioses todavía.

But if the image of the circle is not the child's hoop but the ring, then it is life itself in its anxiety to persist. From the *tercos abrazos* one progresses to *"enjoyar de anillos al poeta,"* when *"Los sumandos frondosos de la tarde/ ... Son en la suma de la noche ceros."* But

> No los ceros solemnes de la nada:
> Anillos para manos de poetas ...
>
> Bajo un rumor de números ardientes,
> Henchidas presidencias necesarias.
> ¡Ceros, ya anillos, fulgen con los astros!

Numbers, but burning. The ring is linked to fire:

> Se queman fiebres y vahos
> Que me ajustan en anillos
> Tiernos soles amarillos.

We have not left the first *Cántico,* but it is in its vital expansion that the poem *Anillo* gives *"fe de vida."* It presupposes the

77

biological cycle of generations, parallel with nature, as is shown by the parenthesis in the third part. An example will suffice:

> Y se encarnizan los dos violentos
> En la ternura que los encadena.
> (El regocijo de los elementos
> Torna y retorna a la última arena.)

The last strophe of this part expresses clearly the image of the ring:

> Alrededor se consume el verano.
> Es un anillo la tarde amarilla.

And, directly, the word *"círculo"* (and its vital reverberations) appears in the last strophe of the poem:

> ¡Sea la tarde para el sol! La Tierra
> No girará con trabazón más fuerte.
> En torno a un alma el círculo se cierra.
> ¿Por vencida te das ahora, Muerte?

This circle is not a barrier imposed by nature, although subject to its law, but created by the conscious desire to love, by the will to love it thus. The lovers, like the pair in *Sol en la boda*; "The two erect, yes, their own barriers."

And when this impulse of life arrives at *Vida extrema,* the cycle is consumed, refined, concentrated, lived through. Thus:

> Más vida imponga así la vida viva
> Para siempre, vivaz hasta su extrema
> Concentración, incorruptible arriba
> Donde un coro entre lumbres no se quema.

Llegó a su fin el ciclo de aquel hecho
Que en sus correspondencias se depura. . . .

But in the correlation between man and universe (the traditional micro- and macrocosm), the visible horizon is the
circle and man himself is the center. In a fuller and more intense way in the noon of *Las doce en el reloj*:

Era yo,
Centro en aquel instante
De tanto alrededor,
Quien lo veía todo
Completo para un dios.

However, this cosmic horizon is not the prison for what is well
delimited. The "rigorous horizon," now almost a pure line, will
open up at the height of perfection, and it trembles:

¡Oh perfección abierta!
Horizonte, horizonte
Trémulo, casi trémulo
De su don inminente.

There is, moreover, a horizon created by the very preoccu-
pations and the very task, as in the specific *Dasein* of Heidegger. And the proper task of the poet is poetry, the "reality"
of which gives him serenity and offers him also a horizon suited
to his liking: *"Justa para mi anhelo/Te diviso,/Horizonte en el
cielo/Más preciso."*

But what about the rupture? Ah, the circle is broken; it
does not open by itself but is opened by grief, sickness, and evil.
Or else the circle is closed, hard, and it imprisons us. It is necessary to go to the last poem of *Cántico* for this conscious, affirm-

79

ative confrontation with the rupture. It happens in the poem *Cara a cara;* its first strophe conveys precisely the image of the circle, but as something that surrounds us oppressively:

> Verde oscura amarillento,
> Deslumbra un tigre. Fosfórico,
> El círculo de agresión
> General cierra su coso.

Here man remains prisoner of the circle that closes around him instead of being opened like the affirmative cosmic circle. We find ourselves in darkness. Therefore, *"Luz urgente de socorro"* is asked. Disorder, shadow, smoke, and storm are cosmic manifestations of the mutation of pain. The "multiple, barbarous, murky" heavens clash.

This conflict—is it essential to being? No, it is accidental. Although *"El agresor general"* is all around, *"Yo no cedo./ Nada cederá al demonio."* Because *"Entre tantos accidentes/ Las esencias reconozco."* More than that: anguish is necessary to feel *"el día realísimo"* and to remain in it, in the center of truth. And the truth is that *"No soy nadie, no soy nada,/Pero soy."* Or rather, I continue to be and to persist in being.

The world thus will be a *Maremágnum* in which the poet finds himself encompassed by a wave *"de veras contradictorio."* *Maremágnum* has an introduction, *El acorde.* And the great harmony breaks: *"El día fosco llega a ser amargo,/ Al buen remero se le van los remos."* It is the rupture of the harmony of the circle by pain, which is non-being. What persists is being: *"Pero el caos se cansa, torpe, flojo,/Las formas desenvuelven su dibujo."* So it is that the circle recomposes itself. It is the permanent problem of evil, if it can be called a problem. Some present-day philosophers and theologians prefer to say "mystery"; an ontological mystery, not theological, is understood. Gabriel Marcel, the French philosopher, has established a distinction between a problem and a mystery.

It is in some short poems—those that express it less directly —that the harmonic curve is most widely broken. It is when something is absurd, and not understood, as in *A pesar mío,* or when the task is difficult, as in *Tácito clamor.*

Not only in *Maremágnum* but also in the other books that comprise *Clamor, Que van a dar en la mar* and *A la altura de las circunstancias,* evil and pain close the circle as a girdle that strangles or breaks the harmony of its cloistered perfection. It would be too much—and not really necessary—to continue giving examples. But the poet, in spite of everything, goes on giving his *"fe de vida,"* his testimony of having lived.

Translated from the Spanish by Bernice G. Duncan

Sail Before the Wind (*Aire Nuestro*)

by Joaquín González Muela

Coplas: *a luz volad.*
Lleváis amor verdadero.

AIR, LIGHT, OPEN EYES, BREATHING have been the solid base of Guillén's physics—not metaphysics. *"Lo profundo es el aire."* From the first *Cántico,* windows and balconies are opened in order to see well or so that the air may fill our lungs; or the blinds may be closed a little so that the siesta may be restful. Guillén has gone on creating his symbol, which has nothing to do with Aeolus or the San Cristobalón of Lorca. We can think neither of an asthmatic reaction nor of a romantic fascinated by a windstorm. It is pure air, that delicious draught that we must now seek far from the contaminated, poisonous atmosphere of our cities. Not only the lungs but also the mind would be grateful for a breath of Guillén's poetical air.

Sometimes he has experimented with the supposed poetic value of words like *auras, rachas,* and *ráfagas,* but the purity of *aire* and *viento* have masterfully prevailed. Muggy lights and stormy winds have sometimes given a pathetic note to *Cántico,* but generally there was an air that was a delight to breathe. This book had to end with *Cara a cara,* where the initial quotation says:

Lo demás es lo otro: viento triste,
Mientras las hojas huyen en bandadas

82

where there is an *"aire cruelmente blando."* But the poem is an affirmation against that, and it contains the phrase:

A la vista siempre aire
Tan ancho tras los cerrojos.

Cara a cara was the final obbligato, but the poet rounds out his book with the preceding composition *El aire,* which is the twilight worthy of *Al aire de tu vuelo* with which the first part begins. In *El aire* he affirms for the last time: *"Y la vida . . ./Es aire, simple portento."* Or: *"¡Anhelo de trasparencia,/Sumo bien! Respiro, creo."*

Let us see what happens in *Clamor* when, in spite of the poet's age, asthma fortunately has not alienated him.

We breathe "fresh air" again (*Nada menos, A la altura . . .*, p. 157), "gay air," (*Mucho tiempo, Que van a dar . . .*, p. 54), "kindly . . . air" (*Reencarnación, Maremágnum,* p. 100), "summer air" (*Vuelo, Que van a dar . . .*, p. 153), "air/Shot through with sunlight" (*Aquellas ropas chapadas, Que van a dar . . .*, p. 39); but there is a serious contrast *"Paredes claras, aire claro, vida abierta . . ."* (*Tiempo de volar, Maremágnum,* p. 172) facing: *"Los monstruos han pasado. ¡Pasado! Se nubla/El aire en que sufren las paredes mutiladas"* (*Ruinas con miedo, Maremágnum,* p. 54). Did the opposition come forth unconsciously *"—paredes claras: aire claro :: paredes mutiladas : aire nublado"?*

The presence of light, which air seems to require, is very frequent. Among various examples, we select this one:

. . . voces nuevas
Que habrán de resonar hacia otros aires,
Aires con una luz

83

Jamás, jamás anciana.
Luz antigua tal vez . . .
                    —*A la altura,* 15

And if it is not air, it is breeze: *"Brisa es luz"* (*Tiempo antiguo, A la altura* . . . , p. 85).

In this poet of liberty, who senses *"El aire/Tan ancho tras los cerrojos,"* it is natural that the fundamental quality of the air be free: *"Aire libre, luz libre lucen dentro/Del íntimo recinto"* (*Forma en torno, A la altura* . . . , p. 20). And more forcefully, the quality of the wind:

La verdad se abre paso día a día,
Entre el agua y la sed,
Entre el pan y las hambres,
Por entre el viento libre y soleado.
                    —*A la altura,* 50

Éramos aventura,
Sólo aventura bajo aquellos vientos

De nuestra libertad mejor creada:
Total amor difícil, siempre en obra.
                    —*Que van a dar,* 99

A free wind, a good wind. The word is not usually loaded with tragedy, with drama. Only once, at the beginning of *Pentecostés, Maremágnum,* it seems to denote a certain sadness:

Un viento de tormenta,
Tormenta sin nublado
De atmósfera,
Encendido fragor irresistible,
Sonó.
                    —*M,* 58

Usually it is a wind good for breathing, which fills the lungs. One example will suffice:

> Y por fin, asomándose a la altura
> Del almenado viento, ¡qué claridades traga
> La ansiedad del pulmón! Recompensa y
>   no vaga:
> Respirar, respirar, la mayor aventura.
> —*M,* 181

(See also *El acorde* of *Maremágnum,* 15, where lungs and wind find they are made for each other.)

Lack of air. Suffocation. Tragedy. They are present in *Clamor.* Let us look at the causes. One is the anguish of love, which strangles the sadly predestined Calisto and Melibea. Calisto in a situation quite opposite to that of the lover in *Cántico,* enveloped in darkness, not seeing or hearing while he is not in the presence of the beloved, exclaims:

> Me hundo en un sofoco
> Donde respiro mal . . .
>   —*Que van a dar,* 181

> Por las cuevas me arrastro,
> Sin aire entre las gentes
> Que nos separan ¡ah! de nuestra noche.
>   —*Ibid.,* 189–90

And Melibea says the same:

> Tampoco yo me conozco,
> Perdida entre los clamores,

Sin respirar en tu aire,
Sin depender de tu noche,
De tu día, de tu sol,
De tu eternidad . . .
—*Ibid.,* 193

In *La sangre al río,* from *A la altura* . . . , it is the confusion
of history, the unlucky circumstances that produce the asphyx-
iation. There is wind, but it is so wicked that it does not allow
one to breathe:

Encrespándose en viento el crimen sopla.
Lo sienten las espigas de los trigos,
Lo barruntan los pájaros,
No deja respirar al transeúnte
Ni al todavía oculto,
No hay pecho que no ahogue.
—*A la altura,* 47

There is much "panting" in that same distressing circumstance
(p. 40). And a similar cause of suffocation, which moves us
to pity, is that of the man unjustly persecuted, the Christ:

Ahoga. La injusticia
Duele al cuerpo también,
Vencido
Desde la sangre al alma.
Ya la respiración es un jadeo,
O apenas soplo de un susurro inerme . . .
—*A la altura,* 28

And finally death, contemplated as usual in Guillén with
complete serenity and naturalness, is the final deprivation of air:

Le dijo adiós el aire. Ya no hay soplo
Que pudiese empañar algún espejo.
            —*Que van a dar,* 12

But in spite of these sad and obligatory negations of vital air, which history or circumstance awards us, in the always affirmative work of the son of Valladolid, the hope for one more breath cannot be lacking:

Si el Poderoso aprieta, no, no ahoga.
Al cuello envuelve un aire
De cumplida esperanza respirada.
            —*A la altura,* 125

Because we already know:

Volver a respirar
es la delicia humilde.
    —*Que van a dar,* 19

And "*Tal dolor, sin embargo, busca el aire*" (*La sangre al río, A la altura* . . . , p. 46).

We have said that Guillén does not follow the traditional symbols of air and wind of the mythologies. But it was impossible to escape the deep-rooted ideas of our culture which for centuries have continued to unite the concepts of *soplo, pneuma, ánima, aliento, espíritu,* and *vida.* On the part of Guillén, there is not in this any proof of a metaphysical cult. The soul has rarely had that aspect in Guillén's works. See how, at the end of *Clamor,* the poet keeps pulling the soul toward the physical area that the senses understand:

Helo, por fin, bien despierto
Frente a frente a la jornada,

Que se extiende por un aire
Pronto a entregar la mañana
Siempre ignota, nunca neutra,
Turbia tal vez o entreclara,
Pero sin cesar atmósfera
Que los pulmones y el alma
Respiran sin distinguir
Entre el aire y la sustancia
Por él difusa, visible
Bajo forma de esperanza.
—*A la altura*, 13

There is even more air, much more air, circulating through *Clamor*. Two entire fundamental poems of *Maremágnum* convey it in the title: *Aire con época* and *El viento, el viento*.

But we must end these comments hastily, and unfortunately we cannot analyze them now. We want to end with some notes on the expression *Aire Nuestro,* which is the title that Guillén desires for his total work. *Aire Nuestro* is free air, our vital food. It is a free gift, the world's gift; but the adjective *"nuestro"* (our) indicates that we must accept it, feel it to be like that exchange of gifts that constitutes the universal relation already expressed in *Más allá,* the first poem of *Cántico.* We must be worthy of this gift:

Era un aire ya nuestro,
Del hombre, de unos hombres,
Aire con una gracia irrepetible.
—*Que van a dar,* 114

That phrase, *"de* unos *hombres"* implies the will to accept the gift—and the possession, once repeated—to which I refer. A tragedy creeps in when we realize that we must struggle to guard that possession. They can take it away from us or try to do so:

Así vivimos sin saber
    Si el aire es nuestro.
Quizá muramos en le calle,
    Quizá en el lecho.
            —*M,* 56

Me distraigo al fin, sonrío.
Pero la angustia me acecha.
¡Si mi aire fuese mío!
      —*Que van a dar,* 74

The terrible thing is that a perverted air is around, threatening us, trying to pollute ours, belonging to others. Already Melibea was sighing: "Without breathing in your air . . . ," and Calisto sees the danger: "And I am lost in the air of others,/ That do not know you" (*Huerto de Melibea, Que van a dar . . .,* p. 188).

And Guillén, who does know, therefore leaves that window open at the end of his work, through which the spirit of a friend breathes:

Mientras haya
alguna ventana abierta.
    Pedro Salinas.
—*Dedicatoria final, Clamor*

May this great work sail before the wind for centuries and centuries.

Translated from the Spanish by BERNICE G. DUNCAN

89

The Long Poem of Jorge Guillén

by Mario Luzi

Jorge Guillén's *Cántico*—I remember well the moment when I heard about it from Hispanist friends and when I myself made its first, still cursory, acquaintance. These were the years when the prestige of Valéry was at its zenith; wherever a powerful poetic synthesis seemed to incorporate a certain intellectual rigor, his work was sure to be evoked.

Guillén's poetry seemed to be following in the trace left by those footsteps. Yet it appeared as an event of a festive nature, which the severity of its model might have foretold, if at all, only in flashes like the *Cantique des colonnes*. Certainly Guillén himself would be the last one to deny that his *Cántico* is a praise intoned by the mythical Valerian intellect which, having overcome the episodic contrasts of that which is, perceives, dazzled, the Parmenidian lucidity of being. This superlative clarity does not conceal the victorious and simplifying operation of intelligence taking place behind the scenes and transforming the arts of the first decades of this century. Nor, in a more specific sense, does it hide the intellectual exaltation which, following the example of Valéry, consents to the vision of the world in full light and to the sensual fruition of its particulars. But to me it seemed that *Cántico* was, in the first place, in its most concrete concern, a song in praise of the real happiness of being, issuing from the plenitude and limpidity of the poet, who is enchanted to be thus and to have thus in his hand the golden key to the world. The metaphysics of Valéry's physics left even in the most fleeting images a strong and acrid sense of dryness and abstraction. In Guillén metaphysics and physics become fused in the fire of a spontaneous, vital intoxication. The liberating power of poetry and of the enthusiastically accepted and affirmed poetic condition assumes, with the heat and astuteness of youth, first place in the consideration of theories of cognition. In short it occurred to me when reading him to perceive a subtle and strong, vital presence, especially when the poet enunciated ecstasy or the admiring exigency of "whiteness" or "absence" as the pure state, conducive to the revelation of the depth of the world.

Later turning his glance from being and from the intuitive interest in the visible toward happenings of history, Guillén confirms, together with his natural strength of assent, the fundamental euphoria of the original image of totality. I know the second, eagerly-awaited book *Clamor* only through fragments and have read with deep enchantment the third, *Homenaje,* recently published. Here the world of essences receives, so to say, the vivacious counterpoint of the world of existence. It does not seem inappropriate to me that the second book figures as a "negative," except so far as injustice is part of the intrinsic justice of the whole. Guillén's inborn metaphysics include in fact an active, moral sense, coinciding with the perfect cheerfulness of his sense of being. It has been said too often that this poetry is a sort of liturgy of the intelligence which has been preserved from the suffering of historic experiences. Instead, it is a celebration at which even evil is present, without being able to interfere. In its successive moments it forms a continuously fertile and acute poem which circles around grace— the revealing and restoring grace of clarity, which more and more identifies itself with maturity and a profound human awareness. In times as dispersive as ours, Guillén has given an example of a firm and mobile poem, tenacious in its foundations, yet not static, illuminated by a primal intuition and supported by long and varied experience. A monument, then, of modern literature.

Translated from the Italian by ASTRID IVASK

The "Clarity in Action" of Jorge Guillén

by FERNAND VERHESEN

FEW SYSTEMS OF POETICS are more open, and at the same time more secret, than that of Jorge Guillén. Few are more simply and directly open to the world (though not precisely to our glance, unaccustomed to perceiving) and nevertheless more hidden from the scrutiny of that world. Infinitely close to things, infinitely distant. Untenable paradox or insoluble dichotomy? And, even so, no work goes farther, continues better; there are few works in which a profound unity appears more dense and indivisible. To reflect on Jorge Guillén's poetic language is to reflect through that language upon the world; and without doubt it is in this very mediation that we find joined the apparently divergent paths of a wholly concrete vision (I mean, centered exclusively on the concrete) and a vision which is wholly mental (that is, exclusively determined through mental re-creation). It appears from the outset that, with Guillén, the image cannot be in any sense the banal interpreter between reality and thought; still less is it to be confused with any suggestive description of reality. Jorge Guillén, in fact, never describes. It is not all through allusion that he evokes or invokes reality, and he never accords it the facility of any symbolic transference. He gives it as itself for what it is, and his poems cite it endlessly under its most diverse and sensitive aspects. He turns toward the external world a patient gaze, tirelessly search-

93

ing. Not to draw up a geographic map or inventory of the real, but rather a mental atlas where reality finds itself caught in the trap of prismatic vision, embodying and recreating what is brought to it. Things told with an apparently perfect objectivity thus take on the progressively living form, captured now by the poet's visual sensitivity, of the inexpressible. We come here to the heart of the paradox: vision does not reveal things, with whatever contained but violent delight, so much as it reveals the missing enchantment of them, or, more often, missing from the instant when they were deprived of their connection with their likeness, on the one hand, and with him who perceived them, on the other. The relations that unify them may appear fortuitous or arbitrary under the imperative of a vision which imposes them from the outside; it is nothing of the sort, and here we touch on what may well be called the metaphysic of Jorge Guillén, the conviction that a dynamic underlying the things of this world regulates their forms as much as does the place of their arising.

On this level is situated what used to be called the inexpressible: the profound directions, the internal pulsations of the elements of the universe, and their innocence also in the face of all the factitious connections that men have given them. Jorge Guillén is the poet of dawn, agreed; but one might as rightly say that he impels into dawn an even earlier light, that light of which we cannot tell at what moment or in what degree it is distinguishable from night. Is it possible, in fact, that there is no night? That perhaps, before they appear to us, things exist in an infra-world which can be penetrated only by what has been called by René Char the *"lumière mentale"*? Actually, the vision of Jorge Guillén is that which promises that mental light. It has been said that Guillén's gaze is essentially auroral; we add: a downward gaze, at least if we hold fast to the norms which determine our habitual position in relation to things. And if the norms must be abolished? Are they not actually abolished from the moment when, instead of considering himself as the reflecting and recreating center of the world, the poet places himself, on the contrary, against that world, even takes at the very center a position of balance, undoubtedly precarious, perpetually within the play of contradictory forces, and makes secure his amazing discovery of earthly realities, seen somehow from the inside, and perceived in their essence? This interiorization of gaze implies that an identical movement was previously in operation even on the human level, but instead of emerging into the "night of the soul," or into nothingness, with Guillén on the contrary it opens (prolonged in the course of a rising asceticism) onto that infra-world, or onto the essence of the real.

A new paradox must be drawn. We say "essence" and we find this in contradiction to certain of Guillén's most peremptory affirmations. "To be," he says: *Ser,* in the poem *Más allá.* *"Ser, nada más. Y basta./ Es la absoluta dicha."* But he adds in the same stanza: *"Con la esencia en silencio/ Tanto se identifica."* The end of the same poem gives us the key to this strange collusion between being and essence: *"La realidad me inventa,/Soy su leyenda. ¡Salve!"*

To be whom? To discover one's own law and to be what is determined by his own joy of being:

Persistiendo en mi ley
Gozo determinándome.

To be that which, once discovered, allows itself to invent from reality, and to disclose his own identity within reality, with regard to which he keeps his distance, refusing to subjectify it but nonetheless apprehending it in an immediate and direct manner, guiding his vision straight to the unsuspected heart of things. This guidance comes after the immediate apprehension (that which is revealed, very often, by the enumeration of objects devoid of any qualification), and arranges the vision according to plans more and more profound, opening sudden perspectives (Guillén's very individual syntax, his ellipses, his significant punctuation)—unexpected perspectives on the essence of things, by which we now see its connection with the being who reaches it, or better, who lives it. If the essence of things can be considered the ultimate reality, it follows that the intelligibility of the world embraces that of its beings, and we are scarcely surprised to see (I say "see" advisedly, for the poet makes us parties to his vision through the mediation of a *Yo,* an "I" who is neither himself nor us, but our anonymous "me") that Guillén writes (in *Más esplendor*):

> ¡Y qué frescura de la lejanía por tu cuerpo,
> Claro cuerpo feliz
> Como paisaje!

From the poem of the object, the vision leads us toward the poem of the beloved being, and we will not insist here on the profoundly sensual aspect (what errors have not been committed in the name of Guillén's intellectualism and abstractionism!) of Guillenian poetry. We are no less surprised by this assimilation of the beloved body into a landscape:[1] it is evidently not a matter of aesthetic contemplation, but more simply, more profoundly, of the natural unity of things and beings, of the total coherence of the world which the glance penetrates to

[1] The similarity with Baudelaire's poem (*À celle qui est tróp gaie*) is surely accidental.

the point of being able, without any intervening image to falsify the relations, to reveal the correspondence between body and landscape.

This is the correspondence intended in the *"Realidad de las Realidades"* (*Más esplendor*), or again *"La realidad en acto,"* which states even more precisely, if there were need, that *"la claridad en acto,"* that is to say, the vision which sanctions this clarity is really the first condition of all investigation, or rather of all grasp of being. It is more a matter of grasp, in fact, than of penetration; we have noted already that the apprehension of being and things was incontestably determined by the notation, often the connotation, enumerative and deliberately devoid of accidental qualification (time is transcended on the same plane on which space is commonly perceived) of elements of reality. A grasp through the vision, a vision which alone justifies the grasping: such indeed seem to be the complementary powers of glance and of mental actualization. These powers will incite us, no matter how we guard against it, to dissolve all tangible reality, to abolish the sentiment to the point where imagination superimposes a disembodied diagram. It is nothing of the sort, and that is why we say actualization and not mental representation. Guillén's vision does not turn toward the unknowable origin of every being and every thing on the emptiness of a prenatal dawn but truly on perfection, on the Perfect where all the conquests of imagination are brought together, revitalized: It is an imagination which *"trouve sa jouissance,"* as Gaston Bachelard said of Eluard, not "in erasing all images" but in giving them body and living substance. This is rightly so because the eye, at first glance, has substituted a deeper view which stabilizes reality and ennobles it. To Jorge Guillén's *Más allá,* his *Más vida* replies proudly:

Hijo, ya impulso hacia la luz
Desde mi gozo:
Hay luz universal
Para tus ojos. . . .

Hijo:
Tu mundo, tu tesoro.

Translated from the French by Constance Wagner

ANALYSES OF SPECIFIC WORKS
II

Time Passes

by PIERO BIGONGIARI

WHILE AN IMAGE IGNITES, time passes. That is, time grates concretely, rapaciously on the shiny, illusory mirror of the archetypal image, and nothing is born but a memory, the memory. It is the product of that futile besieging of the archetypal image. Memory is pain, end, death, and all that is opposed to the image, thus exalting even more its illusoriness and invulnerability. But it is, on the other hand, exactly the fleeting, experimental, casual part—the besieging part—of the memory that stabilizes the transitoriness of the image, which consequently consists of a final invariable. It constitutes its own essentiality, its own essence, real through the frailty of all experience which attempts the whole probability of existence. The essence of existence, it follows, is its supreme improbability; in it experience becomes image, separation of the supreme primary moment, separation of this moment. But in it also the image conceals its own origin, in other words, conceals God. An essential battle goes on between non-being and being; the image, inasmuch as it separates itself as image from its supreme unimaginability, also accepts its temporality, its spatiality. Therefore it accepts the fact that time and space, and the human passion uniting them, close the source of being in order to open that of existence.

The image of Guillén is consequently, in its supreme luminosity, an ambiguous image, *à double face*—an image which cannot turn around toward the face, as if shrouded, of the hidden God, of God betrayed by the supreme human imagination which needs to hypothesize the invisible in order to realize the supreme, necessary affirmation of the visible. But then even the visible suffices no more when it is proved *more geometrico*. The visible, the visible passion of man, consumes itself, is destined to consume itself in a peremptoriness always both final and outdated, down to the archetype, to the separation, the initial severance. In this way poetry, and the poetry of Guillén, while centralizing man as the perceptive moment, also compels man to follow an opposite route, to reverse his own sense of perception, which then becomes more centrifugal the more it hypothesizes its own centricity of perception. The more man seems to abolish the exterior world for his own interior order, the more the world and things exist. By this he has attained nothing but his own supreme dubiosity: while he finds himself, he also loses himself. It is the opposite process to that of Dante's *Paradiso,* where in the *candida rosa* the blessed ones are to be found who appear to the pilgrim-poet's perception, placed at different degrees of perfection, *et pour cause,* in order for him to be able to approach them in his own imperfect teaching. Not so for Guillén. The choirstalls are, for him, in reality occupied till eternity by the infinite human *gradatio,* which the image negates but at the same time conceals. This unending corporeity of the Guillenian being redeems and nearly cauterizes itself in the continually completed Platonicity of the image. And Guillén's *Commedia,* his *Cántico,* is a *Commedia* in reverse.[1]

The *candida rosa* of the fulminous image is nothing but the teaching of the so-called *"poeta puro"* in order to reveal a reality echeloned on the highest steps of infinity: a replete

---

[1] The *Commedia* of Guillén that Oreste Macrí alludes to in *Due poemi di Jorge Guillén* in *L'Albero,* Vol. XIII, (1966), n. 41–44.

infinity, which the "empty" thought accosts with the proper "emptiness," one might say vanity, in order to understand that last fullness. But for the pilgrim, for the *peregrinus mundi, ocioso, caminante,* God is necessarily concealed; if God were to appear, the pilgrim could not fulfill his mission, that is in an *Homenaje* to multiply the quality of being, to make it interminable, innumerable, in order to be able to grasp it with the last quality, emptied and "thought through," of the image. The image, finally, conceals God himself with its supreme transparency. The archetype is not archetype if it is not both negated and affirmed by its infinite multiplication.

I have in my possession, among other valuable Guillén papers, the series of autographs that resulted in the poem *Visto y evocado,* composed November 13–14, 1958, and first published in *Historia Natural* (Madrid, Palma de Mallorca, Las Ediciones de Los Papeles de Son Armadans, now in *Homenaje, 2 Atenciones* II, p. 162). I transcribe here the four pages of manuscript in order to add some observations:

The first page:

> *Visto y evocado*
> *Visto y recordado*   (Florencia, Wellesley)

> Van cayendo las hojas amarillas

> Las hojas, ya amarillas, van cayendo

> Amarillas, cayendo y van las hojas

> Cada cinco segundos, una a una.

> Sobre llovida piedra. Frondas rojas
> De otoños—los recuerdo—ya profundos.

Alma, ¿ya no habrá nada que no escojas?

Second page:

Amarillas, cayendo van las hojas,
Una por una, cada tres segundos
Sobre el llovido asfalto.

Frondas rojas

De octubres que recuerdo, ya profundos.
     ¿Todo lo quieres, alma, nada arrojas?

     ¿Todo lo guardas, alma, nada arrojas?
Alma: ¿todo lo sabes (corrected above to:
     salvas), nada arrojas?
          Florencia 13—Noviembre—1958
          Jueves—Madrugada—Mañana

Third page:
     Visto y evocado

(*Florencia, Wellesley*)

Amarillas, cayendo van las hojas,
Una por una, cada tres segundos,
Sobre el llovido asfalto.

Frondas rojas

De octubres que recuerdo, ya profundos . . .
Alma: ¿todo lo salvas, nada arrojas?

Fourth page:
Una por una, cada diez segundos

cada seis

Florencia—14—Noviembre—1958
     Madrugada—Sábado—(corrected between
          lines to: Viernes)

The explosive quality of the Guillenian image unfolds in a *movimiento lentísimo* until, acquiring rational force, it nearly divides into its imaginative components. The *movimiento lentísimo* and the fulminous *ralenti* of the development show in filigree how the image constitutes the very nucleus of the atom necessary for the memory to constitute itself and for it to move toward evocation which removes the memory toward the depths of being. Here autumns are defined as Octobers; that is, they become more precise in a more closely defined, temporal setting. Observe how the stone washed by rain turns into asphalt, revealing the tenebrous and lucid magma of its depths. The stone is more colored, serene in Florence, shining with an inner light that the rain exalts to starry azure. The asphalt, meanwhile, places itself as a tenebrous intermediary between the yellow leaves which fall and are swallowed up in its murky magma, and the red leaves of the Octobers remembered by the poet. Those leaves were of a blood-red color, existential as the *"sangue raggrumato sui rami alti, sui frutti"* in the *Anniversario* of Montale. Happy mornings, when a thread connects Florence and Wellesley! In the depths of the autumns, and therefore of the Octobers, memory moves like those yellow leaves, which hence, rather than being refused by the soul, are precisely saved by the soul, almost as if they were a flutter of its wings. But what has happened? What brings salvation? It is a memory that has broken the bounds of memory and reaches the mystical, that is the mysterious, depths of the soul, extending the mere perceptible dimensions. Above memories that dream of lost reality, Guillén invents *"El sueño que rememora,"* the dream which remembers reality to come, concentrated through the mediating imagination in its infinite dispersion. The past also occurs in relation to the center of the wheel which is represented by the present. Memory, which is the necessary decentralization, becomes evocation in this passing through the center which is the present and in its extension, both equal and contrary, in the future where it becomes imaginary. The abyss, *el llovido asfalto,* is this: an imaginary diaphragm of the infinite variety of being, which becomes one inasmuch as it is in its supreme proliferation of forms, *". . . el presente ocupa y fija el centro/De tanta inmensidad así concreta."*

I recall the poet's words in *Al margen de Lucrecio* and I apply them to his poetic research, *"Movimiento lentísimo recorre/Bien previstas etapas forma a forma."* Let us measure this poetic hourglass which in its turn measured the flutter-fall of the wings-leaves in those bewitched Florentine mornings. This is the task of the poet-metronome from form to form: in scanned seconds to find the measure of the *movimiento lentísimo.* And we will see that the poet watches the leaves fall, the yellow color standing out against the brown of the asphalt, catching fire from the leafy red of the memory in the soul that evokes and saves, saves because it knows (see the variant *sabes-salvas* on the third page), every five seconds, which later become three, remaining three for awhile only to become ten, and hypothesize themselves in six. This is the definitive test: ten seconds. Let us say that the poet clocks on his chronometer an unrepeatable record, the extreme tension of the *movimiento lentísimo,* the slowing down of quantity to the supreme quality of being, the unchanging figured to the limits, ten seconds, of the continuous change of becoming. Thus poets lose, or gain, their dawns until mornings, and Thursday becomes, without a break in continuity, Saturday, skipping Friday, if by force of seconds, Galilean seconds, the eternal is won, and the illusory calculation of everyday time is happily lost.

Translated from the Italian by ASTRID IVASK

Variations on *Homenaje*

by Ricardo Gullón

Homenaje BEGINS WHERE *Clamor* ENDS. It is a beginning which is both a continuation and continuum, further exploring the themes of *Clamor* but under different light and in new perspective. The poem-titles depict life as creation, recognition of oneself in the poetic experience, and an understanding that poetry is found in and is the voice of the silence of intuition.

From *Cántico* to *Homenaje* the poet has maintained his initial identity, holding fast to that original being. Life has not changed him; it has only stabilized his identity. He reiterates without repetition, in unceasing variations on a theme which is both singular and multiple, atemporal and immersed in existence, in the current that flows to the sea, which is life.

And in the sea abound both lives which crystallize in creation and living words which continuously generate poetry, including the word of the poet himself. From Genesis to Jorge Guillén myriad images fly, lighting up the world, creating it with the radiance of words. Words show the true profile of the land and, at the same time, its mystery; the world is expanded: *"por claridad regala más espacio."* Guillén brings light and song, the chord which harmonizes everything, even disharmony, the rhythm of that which lives in the poem, enjoying a reality and consistency more lasting than life itself.

Upon completion of such a felicitous project. (*Aire Nues-*

tro), begun fifty years ago, Guillén, to us, has become what he imagined Lope to be: a creator of balance in a consummately calculated harmony—a perfect harmony between being and living, light and darkness, the familiar and the mysterious. While some contrasts do exist, they are difficult to substantiate. In the final analysis *Aire Nuestro* is a prolonged attempt to overcome contrasts. Guillén does not deny differences, but he goes beyond the limits which they impose. For the poet, *being* is a desire for self-affirmation, revealed in the natural joy of existing in the world, of understanding and communicating with all and everything around us. Now that it is completed, we see that this work is fashioned in connecting links, essence-existence-essence, in a recurring pattern:

> Si dioses ya me esperan tras la tumba,
> ¿Nuestra muerte despoja de sentido
> Final a nuestra vida y su torrente?
> Que el esfuerzo domine tal balumba.
> Lanzar me baste al curso del olvido
> La intención de ser hombre dignamente.
> —*H,* 71

Without either engaging in a search for the absolute being or resigning himself to considering it as nostalgia for complete unity, Guillén withholds his assent to one of the hypotheses of Heidegger: not the one which sees man as situated in time but to the declaration of man as limited in his being for death. The spirit of the above-cited poem, written in a Goethean vein, is man himself, the being of man, who *in* endeavor and *of* endeavor is shaped. Another poem, after the style of Quevedo, indicates the feeling of Jorge Guillén: life is not captivity, nor is the world a prison in which the perfectability of man is annulled. Neither is life merely a parenthetic sojourn between the womb and the tomb. Life is doing more than dreaming. Thoreau suggests the answer—our daily awakening is an incitement to renew ourselves, to continue being and doing, persisting and persevering.

That this idea of the poet runs counter to current trends is obvious; to understand it fully we usually experience a brief period of disorientation and critical insecurity. Concepts useful in explaining contemporary poetry do not apply, generally, to Guillén; applied to his poetry, they distort and may deform it. His work is deeply rooted in circumstances and history, beginning with a profound vision which includes the circumstantial in a vast and complex totality. Therefore Guillén can hope against all hope and create vital, optimistic poetry. His work is not derived from pretense or dissimulation; he contemplates reality as it is and feels sorrow and perhaps even bitterness toward it. But if nothing human is foreign to him and he is not insensitive to anything, why deny himself hope, open-eyed hope, based on the certainties of daily life and creation?

This work is his defense and proof, the justification of his being, for himself alone and for all the world. Poetic materials, according to Guillén,

> Transmiten una luz
> Que acrece nuestra vida y nos seducen
> Alzándonos a espacios aireados,
> A más sol, a universo,
> Al universo ignoto.
>
> —*H,* 147

This light would not be sufficient without Guillén's inner light, which transfigures brilliance itself and converts it into imperishable substance. In this fashion he saves himself and also saves us through a miracle of form and poetic transfiguration, creating the perfect circle, the rose which is all roses and the day which is always dawn. Salvation is attained through the power of song, converting absence and silence, memory and dialogue into a verbal fabric which, if it does not preserve them in their entirety, at least exalts them, making them the substance of a higher plane, crystalline, solid, and invulnerable to time: The Poem.

The originality of his "dream-creation theory" (*"He de soñar con los ojos abiertos,"* p. 187) is seen in a single technique when the dream becomes life and commitment. It is this commitment, this poetry, which endures, like the imaginary mistress when her lover-inventor ceases to be. Two great temptations of our time, despair and obscure meaning, are avoided in this lyric poetry—poetry that seeks freedom to breathe, without resignation, without panting. For this reason Guillén has never been "in vogue," as were Lorca (perhaps for the wrong reason), Dámaso Alonso, Aleixandre, Cernuda, and now (should I say, "unfortunately"?) Antonio Machado, a poet who, like Guillén, seemed invulnerable to vogues.

Guillén has not given in to anguish nor to systematic negation. His outcry is not in the desert, nor is it fixed by limits; it is interspersed with the consolation of untainted song. Without understanding this process, the reader will never comprehend how Guillén could arrive at the balance and serenity he so admirably achieves.

In *Homenaje,* however, distance seems to be different. But is it, really? The poet continues to speak from the heart, but he feels his voice blending in and participating with other voices—voices that sing individually yet in unison, diverse parts of a whole. For Guillén it is possible to achieve unity without breaking or negating differences which ennoble the individual. Guillén's poetry is born from the fragmentation of the *yo,* and the poem documents that separation. When Guillén selects and annotates poetic quotations, epigraphs, or images, he is setting the stage for an understanding of his own lyric creation. The frequent *yo*s throughout his work, while echoing other voices, also reveal parts of Guillén himself, singular and innumerable, uniform and contradictory. In a thousand voices this fragmentation of conscience is recognized and is gradually integrated by his poetry as a whole.

Although the poem is a testimony of that division, it is also the means of overcoming it. The unifying nature of language is joined by an impulse toward communion, which illuminates Guillén's images and themes. This unity is brought about by love, or rather, in the love poems, where the experience of the poem dominates and transforms the actual, living experience —if it was truly lived. Are things exactly as the poem suggests? Does or did the experience of life's fullness come from everyday reality? I do not know. The poem simply says:

> Amor, amor, inspiración y juego.
> Se sabe y se improvisa. Relaciones
> Placenteras, ahora necessarias,
> Surgiendo van del ímpetu inocente.
> Y embelesados somos, somos, somos.
> —*H,* 265

These lines, echoing others from Guillén in which dawn is announced, transport the reader to the crucial moment of lyric poetry—the moment in which all things brought together by the dawn take form and presence. The self, both he who writes and he who reads, is discovered in the splendor and the surrounding objects. One's relationships with others begin precisely at this moment.

For many, dream is self-absorption, self-confinement in an immensity populated by ominous shadows. In the oneiric world other people are merely a projection of the dreamer, "vain" apparitions, empty and devoid of individuality. Life, in a dream, is only phantasmagoria. Guillén counters this tendency (which I have called a trend of contemporary poetry), by using a calm, courteous voice, by not shouting. He projects a refreshing poetry which in *Homenaje* finds confirmation and which materializes in surprising balance between dynamic and static expression. The poet balances dynamic, vital expression and the calmness of the abiding life. The hours for Guillén—we already know this from *Cántico*—are exact. He deals with definite time, not that of anguish but that of serenity, even though the first is not negated, nor are its causes.

That love should be the force which stimulates joy and a longing for life is natural. Love, here, now, and forever, exalts and enraptures. Into the face of self-absorption Guillén hurls the rapture of amorous life, the one element which makes existence tolerable. Rapture, extending oneself in search of another, demands a speeding up of vital time which Guillén expresses with perfect precision in the frequent use of the word *más*.

In *Homenaje* there is a beautiful variation on the love theme, which I quote in its entirety:

Ojos cerrados, quieta,
Absorta, concentrándote,
Irradias atracción
Desde ese ya silencio
Del ser más inmediato
Que se da, se abandona,
Gentil, a su quietud

Soberana, potente,
Y me absorbes, me absorbes,
Presa, mi presa . . . Tuyo.
                    —*H, 269*

For Guillén self-abandonment is delivery, and concentration is illumination; all result in the natural ambiguity and complexity of love, a single giving-delivering of oneself. It captures the lover as well as the loved. The last word of the poem is not that of the conqueror but that of the conquered: "*Tuyo.*" Summarized as succinctly as possible, the image is no less exact: nothing is lacking, neither the description of he who "*se abandona,*" nor the careful selection of the adjectives—*absorta, gentil, soberana, potente.* The impression of serenity and the naturalness of the act is achieved by the continual development of the poem in the stanza and of the stanza in the phrase, which is all one in the first eight lines of description. Then in two lines the key is given. The pause between the eighth line and those that follow is necessitated by both logic and the need to breathe. Then suddenly, in an extremely efficient contrast, without presentation, without circumlocution, the poet enters into the poem and, in a manner of speaking, becomes its protagonist. Until this moment he has been at a contemplative distance, like a painter in front of his model. In the ninth line he bounds into the picture, submerges himself in it, and pauses from contemplative immobility to participating movement. The rhythm of the poem is accelerated and then reduced to the repetition of a verb which expresses the action of absorption and a noun which indistinctively applies to both the poet and his creation:

Y me absorbes, me absorbes,
Presa, mi presa . . . Tuyo.

This is, if you will, the elemental exclamation, the culmination in reality of the man who could not be a *"tu"* (for her) without first being a *"yo."* In absorption he instantly achieves being.

Space unites and reduces itself to the minimal enclosure capable of containing all life—space where harmony has been established by the relationships of the instant to eternity. Time and space unite harmoniously and a music sounds, not so much from the words themselves but from the relationship beyond them and expressed by them: *"pleno acorde."* Man in his entirety has achieved harmony, and his most revealing word is another key to Guillén's vocabulary: *"gracias."* Thanks to the one who completes him, to the one who relates to him.

It is evident that in *Homenaje* word and deed have an indirect meaning suggested by the title. The poems written in the style of other poets are a declaration of thanks. Also expressions of gratitude are the kindnesses dedicated to those poets, the resemblances and remembrances, and the variations that are not translations but transfigurations. In Guillén these homages reverberate in Spanish as a fulfillment to poets of other languages.

Let us recall the subtitle of *Homenaje:* "A Gathering of Lives." A gathering to which the guests of *Clamor* are not invited. Neither are Lucifer nor Pérez, the potent one, so easily recognizable. With few exceptions, only known creditors are allowed to enter. And how well they are repaid with the banquet served them! Calderón in Segismundo, Pascal in his own shadow, Tolstoy in the dying Ivan Ilyitch, Bécquer among his swallows and honeysuckle, Mallarmé transformed by eternity into the improbable entity called Mallarmé—and all, like him, transformed into myth, corroborated, and contradicted. With each one comes a part of his world and the worlds which through him are integrated into the creation of Jorge Guillén —from the silence of Genesis to the "clear afternoons by the Duero" of Antonio Machado.

Guillén's homages dramatically expand poetic space. The universe fits into a nutshell. Each guest brings his past and present to the gathering, his geographic as well as his purely lyric space. This multiplicity enters into the unity which Guillén imparts to all with the vigor of his style, an element which can unify without destroying already established diversity— diversity that creates unity, not merely a monolithic but also a meaningful, perfected whole.

It has been said, and still may be said, that the poet should be the voice of the universe. While this affirmation is something of an overstatement, it is still acceptable, I think, if it is reduced to slightly less pretentious terms. Wouldn't it be enough to consider the poet the mouthpiece of a collective imagination? Guillén approaches testimonies lent by other poets, assimilates them, and obliquely incorporates them into his own work. Although these homages do not offer the reader the whole universe, they do provide for him a limitless space—open and resounding with a thousand chimes, where it is possible to fly in peaceful safety.

This is the central idea in Jorge Guillén: fly, fly, fly on wings of joy through existence, assured of being completely alive and convinced that life is for life itself and for hope. There is no Dionysiac drunkenness but, rather, a brilliant drunkenness, an exaltation produced by the realization that life is possible. In and of itself life has value; it has meaning and fulfills itself beautifully in the present, in the presents, in the continuity of existence. Several years ago Dámaso Alonso pointed out the determining, joyful nature of song, especially of Guillén's *Cántico*. It is this aspect which causes the poet to march counter-current, in countertime. *Homenaje* continues in the same direction taken by *Cántico;* it is a book of completed experiences and spiritual and intellectual vigor. It negates chronological time and in the negation firmly maintains its identity; it is a work of ascendant, crowning maturity. Rising to the placid waters of love and serenity that constitute the essence of *Homenaje,* one discovers the nearly hundred pages so aptly entitled "The Center." Here the reader finds inspiration and development similar to those of the poem just analyzed, along with, in unforgettable lines, the substantiation of Guillén's characteristic lucidity. This causes the poet to cry out, finding himself lost in *"la nocturna congoja de un desierto,"* sensing behind him the threatening *"jadeos hostiles, aliento/de algún animal violento"* from caged animals that could easily be the same ones that howl in the distance and depths of the elusive Antonio Machado.

Guillén does not deny the threat of pure passion; this must be recognized and frankly admitted. He does not deny the threat; he overcomes it. Continuation of life is possible by overcoming shadows which are filled if not with threats, at least with enigmas. The poet and the man hold fast to time which, being historic time, is really personal time. It was undoubtedly so in *Cántico,* but the subtitle of *Clamor—Tiempo de Historia—* seems to suggest something else. In *Homenaje* time is a tower (p. 297), a vibrating bulwark, announcing the light and life that will come with the day.

Catastrophic climax, the apocalypse, possible and even probable in a "tomorrow" which might actually arrive, is basic to the poem. It does not evoke the tears of Jeremiah or of hopeless rhetoric but the elegance and sobriety to which Guillén, almost solely, has accustomed us:

I

Un fin de mundo anuncian
Gárrulas voces crédulas.
Va a ser, y con nosotros,
El fin.
  —¿El fin del mundo
Para siempre jamás?
—Los átomos, los átomos.

II

Dormía, desperté,
Y mi cuerpo rehecho,
El alma serenada,
Murmuran:
  Bien moriste,
Resucitas, vivamos.

III

¡Cuánta profunda vida tras un sueño!
Va a ser el acabóse. Por de pronto,
El mañana comienza esta mañana.
    —*El mañana,* 298

The delightful second line with its accented adjectives evokes the murmur of voices in a slightly ironic tone that underlines the horror of a prophecy not at all improbable in the dramatization of the event. The sketchy dialogue takes us from the Apocalypse to Los Alamos, a mighty but very real jump. The stanza terminates but without completion, allowing for the hope which in the next stanza is resolved in the expected antithesis: the end that was—and will be—a nightmare. In such a state *"el alma serenada"* and the *"cuerpo rehecho"* find consolation in recognizing as a bad dream that which so many experts diagnosed as unavoidable reality. Everything is stated with rigorous summary; the transition from one state to another is expressed with energetic economy: *"dormía, desperté."* Nothing more—the two verbs of the second stanza are succinctly connected in the phrase and swelled by the implicit meanings in the actions they express. One is static, the other, dynamic, and together they reveal a spontaneous event, that which takes place without intervention of will.

With the exception of the final brief stanza, which is not a conclusion but a reflection, passiveness, or moral reflection, is the characteristic mood of the poem. It invokes Ganivet's *"eje diamantino,"* around which the poetic creation of Jorge Guillén revolves: *"El mañana comienza esta mañana."* I doubt that any other poet in the crisis period of recent years (it is thusly called, for it truly is a crisis) has formulated an identification so simple yet so comforting with regard to man's today and tomorrow. Guillén accepts the present as the future—a tangible future which unfolds, making and using itself up in the hands of man as he lives it. Living in the present, we live in the future. As we read in another poem: *"La Tierra es gran aventura"* and creation, a sheer marvel.

Here are creation and re-creation in unceasing variations. Themes, anecdotes, happenings from memory and from poetry, fantasy, and history bloom together in *Homenaje*. From the theme of the original sin to the descent into hell, all is here: the honest miracle of the golden legend and the idealized passage from the *Romancero* or the *Comentarios reales*, the cruel episode narrated in a certain report presented to the Council of Spain, or—outside Hispanic history—the assassination of Kennedy in Dallas.

I do not believe that Guillén's selection of themes follows

a system. But neither is that choice left to chance. Here, reborn and recreated, are identical themes from earlier poetry. In a certain bygone moment they affected the poet as significant realities, with lasting meaning, intuitions of something which illuminates some facet of this being, *"ondulante y diverso"* (Montaigne), which is man. And they continue to so inspire him.

Myths are vitalized; it is natural that the poet returns and confers upon them the civilized tribute of re-creation. When the poet realizes his own debt to myth, he becomes a contributor, a participant co-operating in the memory and actualization of myths. Inspired by and identifying with them, Guillén infuses these myths with new life, more life, as he would say, reactualizing them for the contemporary reader. One of his methods of keeping current as a lyric poet consists of bringing the pages of *The Aeneid* and the *Divine Comedy* up to date, an impressive testimony of permanence in change—proof of the continuity in time, of similar obsessions and identical ideas. Narcissus and Cain are as alive today as they were yesterday, and they are alive with the actuality of eternity, with that which persists as long as man exists.

A poem, as I have already stated, is in itself an experience, not merely description of an experience. When Guillén makes a poem, finding inspiration in someone else's artistic experience, he points out the affinity and identification among poets throughout all time. Man, like myth, is one, and the variations in presenting him poetically are a consequence of the form which the experience is given. The six compositions in the section dedicated to Narcissus best illustrate the emergence of order and meaning within the space created by the poetic word. The reader already recognizes the characteristics of the figure; he anticipates them while the hero is still a hazy reality in the world of myth. The lines subtly reconstruct the original character and perhaps even contradict him. Variation is, of necessity, difference, and in the new profile a distinct experience emerges, intense and intact. Because of its own intensity, this experience seems to be, or to reduce itself to that which is, essential, definitive, and supreme in the myth. Such an essence is the result of the will—or necessity—to register in the poem an unchanged revelation, a truth which asserts itself over accidents and mutations. The poem reveals and preserves both the event and the imagination, the possible and the impossible. A metaphor is not only an imaginative way of presenting reality but the creation of a reality in which opposites are reconciled in a unity of meaning which illuminates something previously invisible, perhaps nonexistent.

Guillén uses the example of Anaxarete to express something much deeper and more transcendent than the original fable normally evokes. The theme is the inability to communicate, lack of speech, and the resultant silence. *"Yo necesito oír una palabra,"* says the character of the poem; *"es todo preferible a la tortura/de afrontar esa nada oscura"* (p. 385). The face of Bibi Andersson (the nurse in Bergman's film *Persona*) is a pathetic reflection of the hostility and horror of the silence imposed upon her by her female companion. In *Homenaje* this section is entitled "Lost Time," but it could just as easily be called (with a different inflection than that indicated by the novel of Martín Santos) "Silent Time," time void of man, a void which myth, yesterday or today, cannot fill.

I do not think that I am distorting or forcing these poems when I read them and interpret the mythical configuraton as an expression of an unending obsession. This is seen in the fable of a lover whose complaints fall only upon obstinate silence and who fashions himself with easily remembered characteristics. Withdrawal into death does not seem any different from

Bergman's nurse when, at the end of the film, she departs on the bus, empty and emptied, with "death in her soul," as dead as Ifis in the last poem of this series. Bergman and Guillén speak with and through images; in different mediums they express similar moods—the tragedy and the impossibility of breaking the sound barrier which isolates man and causes permanent frustration in the artist.

Was it always so? No, not if we think of the inspirations grouped in the first part of *Homenaje,* nor according to the translations and integral variations of the fifth part of this volume. Everything in *Homenaje* blends together as a result of another tone and feeling, even though such appearances may emerge in a new word, one whose re-creation is a new form. Translation is perhaps the fairest service that one poet can lend another, not only because the art of translating is itself homage and analysis but because it causes the original intuition to glitter with new and multiple radiance. When a second poet illuminates an already existing poem, he brings out lights and hidden corners in a new manner, enriching as much as transforming. In the five versions of the short poem *Glicinas japonesas* (p. 382), we can easily see how changes in the form affect feeling and actually create four different poems (the first version, in prose, seems to be literal). Change of meter and rhythm alters tone and expression.

When referring to Guillén's translations, I dare not generalize. Some, like those of Shakespeare and Wordsworth, are excellent; but, in my judgment, the Spanish poet surpasses himself when his remarkable creative ability takes greater liberties. However beautiful the variations on *Realeza* (Rimbaud) may be, I still prefer the four on Valéry's *La dormeuse*. All four, in my opinion, are not only equal but superior to the original. It is Valéry himself who benefits from the translations and variations made by Guillén. What in Valéry was logic and ideology in Guillén is transformed into pure lyricism. What in Valéry was a problem in Guillén is a mystery:

> Un alentar en sueños, un silencio:
> Invulnerable calma.

Or, expressed in one short Alexandrine:

> Soplo, ensueños, silencio, calma nunca vencida. . . .

Which is not contained in the hendecasyllable:

> Soplos, sueños, silencio. Se desliga
> La paz.

Or, if we prefer, in octosyllabic ballad form:

> Ese alentar, los ensueños,
> El silencio: ¡qué tranquila
> Tregua invencible!

The reader may choose, without mistake, all four images of beauty, breathing in the peace of sleep; each is equally expressive and attractive though not identical. The change of inflection acts on the soul of the reader, becomes more flexible in the looseness of the first variation, expands and blossoms in the Alexandrine sonnet, is stimulated and comes to life in the ballad, and purifies itself in the perfection of the final sonnet, classical in its rigidity, braked in its impulse, but probably the most helpful in abridging the preceding variations. Grace increases in the poem, which gives of itself until it becomes both varied and unified in expression. The word is both the experience and the poem; it gives meaning and life; everything is subordinated to its spell. Feeling and thinking are realized in the word and even depend upon it for life.

The circle closes: *Homenaje* ends where *Cántico* begins. The poetic world of Jorge Guillén is artfully constructed and the work, conclusive, perfect, intense; written for eternity.

> Hemos llegado al fin y yo inauguro
> Triste, mi paz: la obra está completa.

There is no place for sadness. The poet has not arrived at this point worn out but, rather, vital with both life and poetry. The emanation from the fountain has given us much; the water flows so pure and fresh that we cannot accept, or even believe, that it will suddenly cease to flow. To close the circle, to "conclude," is to leave oneself open to new explorations, even after achieving what seems almost impossible—the creation of the "perfect mystery" in the "perfection of the circle." Guillén radically breaks with the poets of night to show us that mystery is more enduring, that it *"refulge y se cela"* in the profound clarity of poetry.[1]

Translated from the Spanish by THOMAS E. LYON

[1] See also Ricardo Gullón, "Rereading Jorge Guillén," *Books Abroad,* Vol. XLII, No. 1 (Winter, 1968), pp. 39–46.

On First Looking into Guillén's *Homenaje*

by Ivar Ivask

WITH THE PUBLICATION OF *Homenaje/Reunión de Vidas,* the Spanish poet has concluded the great design of his life work called *Aire Nuestro,* which embraces also the two earlier books *Cántico/Fe de Vida* and *Clamor/Tiempo de Historia.* A song of praise, a lament over the destructive side of history (but also an appreciation of its positive values), a homage to admired fellow men—these are three fundamental attitudes, three possible uses of the human voice, Guillén's *vox humana.* Together they form a marvel of architectural unity—almost the realization of Mallarmé's *Book* and without parallel in twentieth-century poetry—*Aire Nuestro.* Is it not the presence of air that permits both human life and speech, grants us the gift of light and colors, and appears to us as an equivalent of spirituality and freedom? Air is the unifying element for the 1,700 pages of poetry, written between 1919 and 1966, which cover the broadest imaginable range and variety of insights, moods, experiences, and poetic forms.

Most major modern poets have sought their inspiration (at one time or another) in the realms of myth, mysticism, prophecy, the occult, the subconscious, and the abnormal. Not so Guillén. The strong lucidity of his profoundly Mediterranean poetry is devoted to daylight consciousness and clarity of thought, to the definite shaping of his feelings, and to a courteous cordiality toward all living beings and things. The humble attentiveness that directs all of his verse demonstrates again and again how much more there is still to be seen, heard, touched, smelled, and tasted while we are still wide awake. Guillén is so busy and delighted with exploring this world that he has had little inclination to pry into the next, which may exist behind the curtain of normal consciousness. One world at a time! seems to be his credo. Not the shadows of El Greco but the luminous atmosphere of Velázquez is the home of his spirit. He is indeed a true Castilian, never tempted by the nocturnal sirens of romanticism —a true Castilian also in the sense that he has dared to pursue his own individual vision of poetry in spite of the adversity of history and against the changing literary fashions of half a century.

Now that the third and final part of *Aire Nuestro* is before us, we wonder how the three parts relate to one another. *Cántico* still remains the heart and center of Guillén's modern *Commedia*. In its courageous affirmation and concentrated purity of style, it could not escape a certain one-sidedness: in order to be the more effective, to burn with greater intensity like the sharp tip of a flame. Like sunrays caught at noon in a magnifying glass. *Cántico* is indeed the life blood of *Aire Nuestro* or, perhaps more aptly, its oxygen. Without *Cántico,* no *Aire Nuestro. Cántico* is like a sheltered garden, but one that is situated amidst the hubbub of the city and the threats of history. The moments of happy union with others and the world around us, which *Cántico* primarily gathers, can sustain us in the more abundant moments of despair and separation. (In a way *Cántico* can be read as a manual against suicide.) It is a series of acts of love and faith that do not come "naturally" but must be won from absurdity so that death may not triumph over life. And let us not forget for a moment that this harmonious result of a constant struggle was carried to completion by an exile away from his own people and his native tongue! Nothing could be farther from naïve, fatuous optimism than the self-disciplined attitude that underlies *Cántico.* The proud Spaniard simply prefers not to shed his tears in public, not to parade his inner torments on every page that he writes. It says something about our age that such a poet could be called—precisely because of his aristocratic courtesy toward his readers—everything from a "cold intellectual" and maker of "dehumanized" verse to a "virtuoso" of abstract *poésie pure.* (Luckily for Guillén he has also encountered, from the very beginning of his literary career, critics of real understanding; but they, alas, do not as a rule compose the official literary histories.)

The negative aspects of history, which constantly endanger every garden of personal freedom and youthful happiness, are evoked more strongly in *Clamor.* In *Cántico,* on the whole, the threats of history echo only from afar, as does the sea in a perfect shell found on a sun-drenched beach. *Clamor* sketches in the shadows of late afternoon and adds the lines and wrinkles which inescapably come to the face of youth. Irony and satire flash in epigrams called *tréboles,* or clover leaves; longer poems comment on politics and the vagaries of contemporary civilization. Autobiography is concretely admitted into the mainstream of Guillén's poetry, not by implication alone as was the case before. Of course, there were immediately critics who with malicious joy pointed out that the older Guillén had at last mended his jubilant ways, in fact had become an engaged, almost social, poet. But why should the poet have persisted with *Cántico* more than thirty-one years and 334 poems? He had made his point, and an old man writes differently from a young one. There is no break in Guillén's attitude toward life or poetry, only a thematic expansion; new modulations are added. It probably must be irritating for an age of change to come up against this Castilian oak confidently rooted in the soil of its initial inspiration.

Homenaje is actually the bridge between *Cántico* and *Clamor*. It draws the widest circle for the poet's interest, sympathy, and compassion. The subtitle *Reunión de vidas* indicates that the poet is only the host, not the main protagonist, this time. The book has five large sections: (1) *Al Margen,* (2) *Atenciones,* (3) *El Centro,* (4) *Alrededor,* and (5) *Fin. Al Margen* contains Guillén's poetic marginalia to texts ranging from the Book of Genesis to works by his contemporaries and his own *Cántico. Atenciones* includes verse portraits from Juan Ruiz to Guillén's friends Salinas and Lorca, travel poems about Italy, occasional poems, and gnomic verse. *El Centro* is dedicated to intimate love poetry. *Alrededor* contains narrative poems of a legendary or historical character, inspired by Vergil, Ovid, and Dante or created by the poet's own invention; *Variaciones* is Guillén's equivalent of translations/imitations in which he pays homage to such poets as Goethe, Hölderlin, Wordsworth, Leopardi, Shakespeare, Tasso, Rimbaud, Yeats, Valéry, Rilke, Montale, Supervielle, Fernando Pessoa, Wallace Stevens, and Jean Cassou. Guillén's celebrated version of Valéry's *Le cimetière marin* (1929) is included. *Fin* presents prose poems, philosophic meditations, the richly varied series *Según las horas,* and several poems that sum up movingly yet proudly the poet's long-sustained effort: *"Este sol inflexible de meseta/Nos sume en la verdad del aire puro./Hemos llegado al fin y yo inauguro, /Triste, mi paz: la obra está completa"* (*Obra completa*). *Meseta* recalls immediately the Castilian plateau where the poet was born on January 18, 1893, and which he mentions, for example, in that poem (included in the 1928 edition of *Cántico*) and in *Cumpleaños*: *"Crea tu amor, eres libre,/En tu meseta ya* arriba" (*Clamor: II, . . . Que van a dar en la mar*). The last lines, *"Yo inauguro,/Triste, mi paz: la obra está completa,"* echo a line from the *Cántico* poem *Vida extrema*: *"Paz: es la obra."* The way the three books of *Aire Nuestro* are interwoven in their imagery and symbolism will take more than one generation of critics to unravel.

The above skeleton outline hardly indicates anything of the body of *Homenaje,* its complexity and scope. This book really challenges into being a civilized society of charm, wit, taste, liberal humanism, courtesy, and grateful friendship. This society —minuscule but real nevertheless—comes about in the magnetic field of Guillén's life and poetry. *Homenaje, atenciones,* and *convivencia* are the key words that all point in this direction. *Convivencia* of friends, ages, countries, literatures, books, and genres. The range has breadth and depth. (Joaquín Casalduero has pointed out that the sections of *Cántico* are arranged like the petals of a rose; the same is true of *Clamor* and *Homenaje*). The whole book seems to be carried by the tone of the poet's voice, animated by his conversation. "Conversations with friends" could be one of the other possible titles of *Homenaje.*

Homenaje is an astonishing catch. The finely meshed net of the poet's attentiveness has caught here an incredible diversity of flora, fauna, and homines. Although chiefly written between 1949 and 1966, the book contains literally a lifetime of observations, reading, and encounters. The origin of the book is very personal, but the total effect transcends the merely personal because the connections and interconnections among all these impressions and meetings are so numerous that they reflect the infinity of life itself, not the life of the author alone. It is not difficult to get lost in Guillén's *Homenaje*—as in an Italian baroque garden with its countless and ever-surprising new vistas, mirroring pools, and fleeting perspectives. Yes, there are actually fountains, flowers, trees, music, promenading couples, disputing friends, illuminated interiors visible from the garden, a lonely reader with a book in a shady arbor. . . . Even falling asleep does not deprive the poet of this essential companionship: *"Es la dulce inmerción, despierta aún la hora/A través de un olvido que no renuncia a nada,/Hacia el sueño cargado de porvenir creciente./Descanso en noche astral, dormiré en universo"* (*Transición*). *"Convivencia"* again, whatever the comparison employed to characterize better this baffling book.

The core of love poetry in *Cántico* is more impersonal, diffuse like the warmth of the sun. In *Clamor* a new kind of love poetry began to crystallize and achieves its culmination in the section *El Centro* of *Homenaje*. Does one dare to reveal that it was written by the poet in his sixties? *"Muy tierno el beso, junta/Sin cesar dos afanes./La respuesta es pregunta."* This love poetry is so deceptively simple yet so full of grace, human dignity. Guillén's Goethean ability to love, and to be reborn in love, is perhaps the real secret of his human and poetic creativity, which are one.

That *Clamor* complements *Cántico* is obvious to every attentive reader. But *Homenaje* adds a needed third dimension to the total design. Only now do we understand that it simply had to be written, for old and new friends alike or, as the final dedication puts it, *"Al amigo de siempre, al amigo futuro."* This collection will always be an intimate dialogue with the living person Jorge Guillén, poet. The reading of *Aire Nuestro* as an architectural, compositional unity will be another new experience even for those readers who are acquainted with all three parts that constitute it. Guillén himself often refers to the admired example of Bach. "Jorge Guillén, the Bach of poetry" is as good a formula as any. However, for us at least, it is the music of Mozart which comes to mind more often when reading Guillén's poetry. No doubt Bach is unsurpassed as an architect of harmony and counterpoint, but Mozart seems more modern: Austro-European, Italianate, Mediterranean, gay and witty, yet fully aware of the Queen of Night, and no less a master of perfection than Bach.

Of the generation of 1898 in Spanish letters, the three great poets Antonio Machado, Juan Ramón Jiménez, and Miguel de Unamuno are safely established modern classics; Jiménez received the Nobel Prize in 1956. The final evaluation of the next generation, that of 1927, is definitive only as far as Federico García Lorca is concerned. Of all the talented poets of this amazing generation, it is, in our opinion, Jorge Guillén to whom the place of honor next to Lorca belongs. Guillén's life work in poetry, *Aire Nuestro,* is an achievement of such durable quality and unflagging inspiration that it deserves to be more universally known. Its author should be by now one of the most worthy contenders for the Nobel Prize in Literature. America can feel honored indeed that she could give asylum for many years to this Castilian poet, who celebrated on her soil his seventy-fifth birthday.

Phono-Symbolism in *Cántico*

(*Critical Fragment*)

by Oreste Macrí

THE RIVER SEEMS the most natural place of happiness for the *distraído* or *vacante*:

¡Alma tarareada goza del río suyo!

It is the last verse of *El distraído* (C² p. 134, C⁴ p. 191). Of the two absorbed ones, the "attentive fisherman" and the "marvelous musician," we are here interested in the musician who discreetly isolates the

La ra ri ra,
    ta ra ri ra,
       la ra ri ra . . . ,

an elemental reduction of the physical language to *"sílabas/Desnudas y continuas."*

Other examples of expressiveness are given in the second *Cántico* as a phonic figure of a new *inmediatez* and an intoxicated *excitación* of more abundant being (*ser más*) which results from direct contact with nature; a phonic figure that reproduces (absolutely) the intoxication of the protagonist in love, even when a root of meaning intrudes into the purely imaginative segment, as in *"Mármara, mar, maramar"* of what appears in being (*El aparecido,* C² p. 263, C⁴ p. 464) a cry of *"ser y flotar,"* a Guillén pattern of *ex-sistencia.* Note particularly a definite zigzag of lightning in the semantic area of raw and intense violence of the patent being: the sea *"díscolo," "silbidos"* of the *"espuma"* that *"Esparcen escalofríos," "formas de ídolos/Recónditos," "irrupciones," "eses de móviles algas," "red de nervaduras/Lívidas"* of the very lightning. Even the smoothness has no repose, it is active; the protagonist emerges *"tajante" "con felicidad de filo."* The appearance of being takes place *"entre dos olvidos,"* almost between two non-beings.

Therefore, the speculative structure of the existential lightning in *Cántico* (contraction of the expectancy of love) is delicate and tremendous in its abolished time that reduces to the minimum, to the limit, the space of *nada-vida-nada,* that is, the vital section of the interval; but to a minimum that is a maximum of domination, just and equitable on occasion (nothing Dionysian here): niche or haunt of eternal dominion, replete and thrown back to a *más allá* of the soul in love, that beyond its former casual dreamlike hell reacts with the *"Mármara, mar, maramar,"* the beginning and closing metric of a chorus phonically progressing by the preposition *con* (*"Vigor de una confluencia* [...] *Confluyan los estribillos* [...] *Cielos comunicativos* [...] *Fluye todo el mar conmigo-/Una confabulación/Indomable de prodigios* [...]." It is *"cantar sin designio,"* like the chirping of the little birds in *Advenimiento* (C¹ p. 12, C⁴ p. 46), *"Sin designio de gracia."*

The swimmer in *El aparecido* is analogous to the "body in the wind" and the bodily *"gloria"* in *Viento saltado* (C² p. 257, C⁴ p. 124); the protagonist with similar free and open metric fluidity belongs to the wind, is through the afternoon more wind, is more than himself (the wind is also love in *Cántico*). Like the explosion of a closed nucleus, in this even more closed poem ("*¡El día plenario profundamente se agolpa/Sin resquicios!*"), like the movement of liberation: "*¡Oh violencia de revelación en el viento!,*" like the domination of the eternal, it is further revealed in the existential sea of *El aparecido*. Analogous to the already mentioned zigzag of the lightning (in *Tiempo libre,* C^4 p. 156, "*el zigzag del pez*") is the sharp closing stroke in the fourth strophe which in C^3 is repeated in the ninth:

> ¡En el viento, por entre el viento
> Saltar, saltar,
> Porque sí, porque sí, porque
> Zas!

(The "*sí*" comes from "*Sí, sí, sí,*" the "word of the sea" in *Más allá,* C^2 p. 14, C^4 p. 18.) The "*Zas*" is the phonic bearer of the noted instantaneous brevity of the vital section, cipher of the eternal, igniting the summit and the sphere of the first *Cántico*; and in effect the leap is made "*a un segundo/De cumbre*"; the feet "*Sienten la Tierra en una ráfaga/De redondez!*"

These phonic, expressive moments of existential motivation are measured out in the aggregate of *Cántico,* rising in a manner neither superfluous nor exceptional above the normal level (being themselves norms) of the general harmonic-orderly texture (alliteration, transpositions, *poliptoto,* popular etymology, monosyllabism, asyndeton, interjection, interrogation, counterpoint and atonality, dominant assonance and consonance, refrain, etc.). The sure, impetuous outbursts of the phonic-symbolic element rebounds from the normal context—menacing as flames, ice, horns, whistles, and double beat rise from the musical texture of *Printemps* by Stravinsky or *Amor brujo* by de Falla. It seems at times as if the text rises by itself, passing to a new transcription after some years: the "z" of "*iza*" in "*que iza en sublime siniestro"* disappears, returning in the zigzag of *"Que hasta el zigzag del siniestro"* within the chaotic combustion (ignition of a chaos) of that yellow night of sleeplessness (*Noche del gran estío* C¹ p. 130, C⁴ p. 184); the last three verses of the first edition (1921) are suppressed so that the unexpected couplet will be more noticeable:

¡Ay, amarilla, amarilla,
Ay, amarilla, amarilla!

In the same way the inert "sinking" of *"es un frágil esquife zozobrante"* in the first edition (1920) of *Buque amigo* (C¹ p. 75, C⁴ p. 312) is expressively sounded in the text of C¹ (1928): *"¿Zozobrará, zozobrará ese buque?"*

Very productive is this asemantic bearer *z-*: "zozobra [. . .] Tiende un silbido" (*Unico pájaro* C⁴ p. 247); "una zozobra/De luz" (*Las cuatro calles* C⁴ p. 409); "Ya invisible y *zumbón*, celeste círculo" (*Gran silencio* C¹ p. 68, C⁴ p. 315); "Más atropelladamente/Zumban ondas. Son, serán" following "silbos y tumbos" (*No es nada* C⁴ p. 322); "¡Cuántas pistas [. . .] zumban! ¡Oh vibración" after "vibran [. . .] rumor [. . .] Silban [. . .] Soplo total palpita [. . .]" (*Meseta* C¹ p. 154, C⁴ p. 491); "un tren [. . .] *zumba* por entre [. . .]" (*Paso a la aurora,* C³ p. 101, C⁴ p. 107); El tren [. . .] Desde los *zumbadores* [. . .] del telégrafo" (*El diálogo* C⁴ p. 129); "A contra luz, algo anónimo/Que *zumba* hostil" (*Cara a cara* C³ p. 384, C⁴ p. 514); "El retintín/De algún cobre/Sobre/Tanta lámina de *zinc*" (*Los balcones del Oriente* C³ p. 263, C⁴ 329); "Amor *zahorí*" (*Mayo nuestro* C³ p. 72, C⁴ p. 88); "este sí/Del pulso [. . .] *zahorí*" (*Afirmación* C² p. 218, C⁴ p. 258); and see also *zumbido, zarzal, zambullir, zumo,* etc.

An expressive example of the *t-* is found in words like

tú, ti, tumba, tumbos, retumbos, tumulto, tropel, toro, etc. We give some examples of significant series. *La vida real* (C³ 366, C⁴ p. 470) is dominated by images of tumult and windstorm, inserted in opportune places: *"exabrupto* [...] *azar testarudo* [...] *abrupto* [...] *¡Qué de tumbos/Y retumbos* [...]*! Dure el tumulto* [...]." The only *"retumbos"* now in *Arena* (C² p. 272, C⁴ p. 482), developing widely the *r-* of the prefix within a phonetic body of classic perfection imitative of the crackling split of the undertow on the sand, the centuries that God, ageless, holds clean before Him in an eternal instant of silence:

> Retumbos. La resaca
> Se desgarra en crujidos
> Pedregosos. Retumbos.
> Un retroceso arisco
> se derrumba, se arrastra.
> ¡Molicie en quiebra, guijos
> En pedrea, tesón
> En contra! [...]

Later the prefix *re-* is added to the same *crujir: "Cruja y recruja* [...]." (*Noche del caballero,* C⁴ p. 425).

Nevertheless, the *r-* yields to the *l-* (*"limpios"*) and to the *s-* (*"silencio"*) with the transition to the pause of silence in the marine echo: *"sin ruido/Sobra la arena, suave/De silencio. ¡Qué alivio,/Qué sosiego! Silencio/De siempre, siempre* [...] *siglos* [...] *Calladamente limpios* [...]." In the last two verses the opposition *r- s-* is epitomized: "Retumba *el mar, no importa./¡El* silencio *allí mismo!"*; from the *"silencio del mar"* must come the quoted *"palabra del mar,"* the *"sí, sí, sí"* of *Más allá.*

In the atmosphere of the *"fragor de creación"* let us examine the difference "rumor/*luz*" in the cited *Paso a la aurora* in the dominant verses: *"Todo en su luz naciente se aligera* [...]

A plena luz la calidad de ser.//Fluye la luz en ondas amarillas"; *"Unánime fragor de creación* [. . .] *barro,//Derrumbamiento* [. . .] *despilfarro* [. . .] *Todo, sí, rumoroso* [. . .] *Se riza de recreo* [. . .] *Madrugador, un tren* [. . .] *por entre el caserío* [. . .] *pro-rrumpe* [. . .] *Un runrún que va siendo rumor de compañía* [. . .],*" with very delicate shading of the two phonic radii:

A través de un aire más libre la luz se atreve.

Examples of the alternation of *r-* with *s-* and *z-* in *Santo suelo* (C³ p. 296, C⁴ p. 364) follow: *"entre los ruidos:/Tren ensordece-dor, raptor en ranchas,/Roncos deslizamientos—o silbantes* [. . .] *bajo los ruidos* [. . .] *Nuestro sosiego nunca silencioso* [. . .] *rumores:/Borrascas por carriles,/Otra vez el desliz/Fugaz*]. . .]."

The *"Se desgarra"* of *Arena* recalls to us the *"Se resquebraja"* of *La tormenta* (C¹ p. 26, C⁴ p. 77): to the *"Retumbos,"* on the pattern of *"tumbos y retumbos"* quoted from *La vida real,* correspond the *"Embates de rebotes//De bronce en bronce"*; at the end of *"Silbos sesgos"* and the syllabic alliteration *"¿Víspera? ¡Viva, viva!"* is almost etymological. A phonic con-stant is the binary method of order alliterated with mutual se-mantic movement (we cite the pages of C⁴): *"cálculo de cólera"* (p. 113), *"profusión furiosa"* (p. 250), *"me arrulla un ruido"* (p. 262), *"palpita con pulsación"* (p. 297), *"late con latido"* (*ibid.*), *"pozo de gozo"* (p. 138), *"óptimo otoño"* (p. 415), *"rompe así la realidad/En mis rompientes"* (p. 522), *"Con su rojo arrulla el brillo/De la brasa"* (p. 431), *"En relámpagos se rasgan* (p. 515), *"Los siseos de algún coche/Que se desliza despacio"* (p. 440), *"Hasta el carruaje veloz/Es ráfaga referida"* (*ibid.*), *"la rotunda red total"* (p. 441), etc. The word is fre-quently repeated with the intention of agreement, cohesion, exactness: *"forma a forma; borde a borde; hoja a hoja; la luz en luz; uno a uno; noche a noche; sesgo a sesgo; días y días,"* etc.; the Biblical type is notable in *"gozo de gozos; realidad de realidades; negrores de negrores; generaciones de generaciones."*

Very important is the reiteration of the *tú* which begins in *Salvación de la primavera* (C^2 p. 90, C^4 p. 92) as a grammatical sign of the first encounter of the beloved with her unique individuality. It is the new truth of the second *Cántico: "¡Amor! Ni tú ni yo./Nosotros, y por él/ Todas las maravillas/En que el ser llega a ser."* Love, anterior to mediation, is the union of *Los amantes* (C^1 p. 36, C^4 p. 37) who have withdrawn from everything:

Sólo, Amor, tú mismo,
Tumba. Nada, nadie,
Tumba. Nada, nadie,
Tumba . . .—¿Tú conmigo?

The lack of differentiation between the two lovers is carried by the *tú* which is referred with affirmative voice to *Amor,* then, with hollow and astonished interrogation, to the unknown beloved. The phonic-semantic alliteration order *tú-tumba* is evidence, rather, of unfolding paraetymological derivation in chiasmatic series of *tú-tumba-tumba-tumba-tú* (the third *tumba* of the first edition in *Revista de Occidente,* 1926, is unlike the explicit *Pero* in C^1, 1928). The new *tú* is celebrated in the last two paragraphs of the cited *Salvación de la primavera: "Un velar/ Fatalmente—por ti//Para que [...] Seas la vida tú."* (The *tumba* will disappear or survive later, differently qualified: *"¿Tumba/ Para una resurreción [...],"* *Pleno amor,* C^3 p. 371, C^4 p. 499.) The *tú* of "seas la vida *tú*" ascends as it is reiterated in the following:

¡Tú, tú, tú, mi incesante
Primavera profunda [. . .]!
¡Tú, ventana a lo diáfano [. . .]!

with sixteen qualifications in a *"letanía a tú"* style (González Muela) as far as *"mía."* The last four lines contract the mediation in discreet and total harmony of the minimum-individual in which the *"Universal"* (*"Universal y mía"*) took shape, multiplying the *u-* in a phonic image of deeply joyous integrity of the vital Eros:

¡Tú más aún: tú como
Tú, sin palabras toda
Singular, desnudez
Única, tú, tú sola!

Note the rhythmic counterpoint *"tú como"* and the triple and continuous carrying of *"como/Tú; toda/Singular, desnudez/Única"*; the expressiveness of the conveying *tú* reaches a maximum within the minimum metric space.

This *tú* moves to the third *Cántico*: the *"casi desnuda"* beloved, girded by *"su estío/Personal"* is enclosed at the end in a *"Tú, fatal"* (*Rosa olida* C³ p. 199, C⁴ p. 253); in *Santo suelo* (C³ p. 296, C⁴ p. 364) the same beloved is the figure in the fatal turning of daily love to a palpable surface (now the love is family and child . . .), also here with the *tú* repeated in the final closing verse:

Tú nos creas, Amor, tú, tú nos quieres.

Let us return to the cited poem *Noche del gran estío*. To the insomniac on his bed of anguish, a deluding meridional light seems to cover the world with a bull's hide; but is it the noonday sun or rather the bull's splendid neck striking the bullfighter, brilliant in his *"traje de luces"* (*"la luz del diestro"*), and dragging him uplifted along to his zigzagging fatal fall?

> ¿Un mediodía . . . : de luz,
> O de taurino testuz
> Que hasta el zigzag del siniestro
> Levanta la luz del diestro?

Worse: it is the *"ignición del caos."* The text of C^1 ends, as we have seen, after the invocation to the wind and to the rains with the repeated cry:

> ¡Ay, amarilla, amarilla,
> Ay, amarilla, amarilla!

Observe that in the first edition at the beginning and at the end the poet asks: *"¿Soy* [. . .] *tu reo?* [. . .] *¿Por qué oh noche soy tu reo/Sin culpa?"* So then, the semantic area of investigation is the following: *toro-fuego-amarillo-viento-agua-reo.* Let us set out on the search.

The reverse of *Noche del gran estío* seems to be *Ardor* (C^2 p. 293, C^4 p. 478): the summer aggregate of stubborn trumpets, sparks, metallic odor, and cruel light has a meaning contrary to the anguished ambient of the previous poem: the *ardor* becomes a sign of reconcentration, of a warm source of being: compact and rounded, the *expectación* is fixed:

> Y en el silencio se cierne
> La unanimidad del día,
> Que ante el toro estupefacto
> Se reconcentra amarilla.

The *"toro estupefacto,"* a reduction of that *"taurino testuz,"* is a solar divinity, light-ardor, or the same *"expectación"* that results from *Su persona* (C³ p. 344, C⁴ p. 492): *"Amarillea,/ Inmóvil, la expectación/Yacente sobre la arena"* (the *"arena"* is the *"redondel"* where the expectation of *Ardor* awaits). We are present at the birth of a myth: the concretized mass of waiting as a natural and human endeavor toward the *más allá,* that is, the instantaneous and at the same time very intense interval, being in movement between reality and more reality (a fable in itself), being and more being, life and more life; the inflexibility and obstinacy of beings in the canicular block is plasticized in this Picasso-Lorquian *"toro estupefacto,"* perhaps more in the Stravinsky manner (*"es la primavera genitora de las estaciones* [...] *henchida del futuro* [...] *mugida por un toro* [...] *esos toros* (of the *Sacre du printemps!*) [...] *mugen con toda sabiduría* (*"Desde París. Falsa barbarie,"* La Libertad, January 18, 1921), whose reflection upon the diurnal ambient is the yellow of copper or bronze (*"metal envolvente"*), kindly and positive, where the yellow of suns and of the night fever in *Noche del gran estío* was negative and alarming; the *t-* is introduced by *"cornetines/*[...] *Tercos."*

The poem *Las llamas* (C² p. 234, C⁴ p. 362) must be contemporary. We remain in the area of obduracy: as under August in *Ardor "Se obstinan profundamente/Masas en bloques,"* so here the flames, whose boundary is the night *"atesorada"* and *"muy noble,"*

> Tanto se obstinan, tanto
> Que asciendo a sus desiertos
> Oro maravillado [. . .],

the golden spark of the inferior burnt material which grows

and attempts to reach the firmament. The *"oro maravillado,"* the heart expanded by fire, is a variant of the *"toro estupefacto"*; in *"maravillado"* there is a play on *amarilla,* a partial anagram of *amarilla* (with the *"toro estupefacto"* in *Ardor* we read *"Alzarme a la maravilla"*). And if gold is not enough, the wind is shown as another erotic *daimon* of the impulse to the beyond and to more abundant being. The wind appears and helps the desire of the flames with its *forma;* it seems that the very flames ask for help: *"Viento,/Aparece, socorre,"* just as in the *Noche del gran estío* the insomniac cries: *"¡socorro!"* to the same wind, with a contrary meaning of anguish.

> . . . Y creándose, torpes
> Manos palpan un cuerpo:
> Toro aún y ya noche.

The other explosive *p-* comes forth. The formula *aún y ya* (studied by González Muela) synthesizes another mythic unit, the *toro-noche.* The alliteration *"torpes* [. . .] *toro"* corresponds to *"tercos* [. . .] *toro"* of *Ardor;* the *tacto* or *contacto* of the hand (a typical Guillenian mediator) guarantees the immediacy of the transition, and above all the indivisible complex *alma-cuerpo.*

In *El sediento* (C^2 p. 68, C^4 p. 74) in a hot desert the help implored by the insomniac in *Noche del gran estío,* whose enemy *"taurino testuz"* returns in the *"toros ocultos,"* is realized:

> ¡Desamparo tórrido!
> La acera de sombra
> Palpita con toros
> Ocultos. Y topan.

The syllabic alliteration *to-* seeks and unites in a prelinguistic musical zone the motivation of the entire semantic area, alternating with *p-* and *ḳ-*. Remember that in Castilian *palpo* and *palpito* are equivalents.

The bulls symbolize the pure negative darkness of childish fear in the third *Cántico*. The child falls asleep, but the oneiric-nocturnal monsters do not disappear but remain substantive, threatening and lying in wait for the present and future man (*Un niño y la noche en el campo,* C³ p. 253, C⁴ p. 320):

> Y el niño va durmiéndose mientras de las tinieblas
> Surgen bultos campales, noche agolpada, toros.

The *"noche agolpada"* recalls to us the *"masas en bloques"* of the Dog Star in *Ardor*. A proof of the alternation *t-/ḳ-* is the *coco,* mythical synonym of the *toro* in *De noche* (C¹ p. 66, C⁴ p. 320): *"Hostil al coco, dócil al encanto."*

Often the triplicate use of words is analytically deduced from the title of the poem, for example: *"-sed, sed, sed-"* of *El sediento,* *"Más más, más"* of *El manantial,* *"De prisa, de prisa, de prisa"* of *El retrasado* (by contrast), *"Sigue, sigue, sigue, sigue"* (quadrupled in the first and last verse with *Vuelta*) of *Sierpe,* almost a poetic totem of words and series in *s-* (*silencio, silbido, siempre,* etc.; cf. *"Siempre siempre, siempre"* of *A lo largo de las orillas illustres*). In the same way the *p-* of *"polvo, polvo, polvo"* descends from *patria* which is the *"Castilla"* of *Luz natal* (C⁴ p. 338), climbing to the semantic field in *p-* (*palpo, palpar, palpitar, pulso, pulsación, palpitación, pulular, Pululación, pisar,* etc., beside *latido, latir, respiro, respirar,* etc.). Such reiteration is asked for by a phonic aggregate in *p-* in the same strophe and the two previous ones: "¡Oh *patria,* nombre exacto [...] Es el *planeta patrio* [...] oh *patrias* juntas! [...] *Para* nuestras dos manos .../Pilas, moles, derrumbes/Y *polvo, polvo, polvo* [...]"; such a phonic series is extended throughout the poem: "Un trozo de universo" [it is "un trozo de *planeta*" of A. Machado, IC, v. 31] "Sin cesar revelándose *planeta* [. . .] *Preciso* ante un confín [. . .] y sin final se *precipitan* [. . .] hasta *perderse* [. . .] los estériles *paréntesis* [. . .] Por *palabras* que son de vuestra boca [. . .] Sustentación de *patria* [. . .] Sin *principio* ni término.//¡Oh *padre* generoso [. . .] A *pie* quieto muralla [. . .] bajo tu *poderío* [. . .] Con el *porte,*/Esa inflexión [. . .] Y la *palabra.* ¡Nuestra la *palabra* [. . .] *Próximos* a sus cielos [. . .] *penumbras* [. . .] Mortuoria ceniza *problemática* [. . .] En esta *pulsación* que marcha sola (here we cite *"patria* [. . .] *planeta patrio* [. . .] *patrias* [. . .] *Pilas* [. . .] *polvo, polvo, polvo"*) *prepotencia* [. . .] *piel* relumbrante [. . .] *poder, pelar* [. . .] *pulula* [. . .] ¡Hermosas *precisiones!* [. . .] la *profundidad* de la mañana [. . .] así *perdura*/ Mi ahinco meridiano [. . .] *¡Problema! Polvoriento/Problema* del inerte,/*Profecía* [. . .] *Problema,* no *problemas* [. . .] ¡Cuántas [generaciones] *pisarán* esta cumbre que yo *piso!* [. . .] Confío mi esperanza a este *planeta*/En su *presente* forma de terruño./ A *pleno* acorde [. . .] *pinares* [. . .] *potencia* guardada [. . .] *¡Primavera* irrumpida! [. . .] Esa *planicie* [. . .] *Paredes* y solaz [. . .] Término de *planeta* nunca antiguo."

The musical constant in *p-* resounds in its various contrasted and interwoven registers, the real, springlike, and profound *patria* being structured against the dust of the ruins, the superiority of race, and the false "problem" of Spain. Geological-astrological registers (*planeta, planicie, pinares, pilas, paredes, primavera, piel, precisiones, profundidad, potencia*), psychological-connotative (*pulsación, pulular, pisar, perdurar, potencia, preciso*) eternal (*sin principio, próximo, presente, pleno acorde*), laral-generational (*patria, patrias, padre, palabra, pie quieto, poderío, porte*), historical-negative between pity and disdain (*polvo, polvoriento, paréntesis estériles, penumbras, precipitarse, perderse*), post-'98-Orteguian (*problema, ceniza problemática, polvo, polvoriento, profecía, prepotencia, poder, pelea*). Nature and symbol are joined at a telluric-animal point, the mythical lion-bull, a figure of the Castilian man, the brute that is basely converted into a man:

> El sí, el no del animal que elige,
> Que ya se elige humano.

Here is his semblance, which recalls to us the Unamunian lion-bison, the knight of Machado, Ignacio by Federico García Lorca (*"Contemplad su figura"*):

> Mirad su catedura.
> Desde el testuz de toro,
> Las crines de un león muy jaspeado
> Por la piel relumbrante,
> Y un sonreír de estío que ilumina
> Boca, dientes y voz [. . .].

The alliteration of *t-, p-, k-*, as opposed to *l-, r-, s-, c-*, has its roots in the *t-* of *toro*, as it more exactly appears in the first strophe cited from *El Sediento*:

> Palpita con toros
> Que ya se elige humano.

The semantic-series distribution is varied and free, as we have seen, but the height of mythic obstinacy is found in this *"testuz de toro"* of the Castilian man-animal, prefigured in the positive and negative of this *"taurino testuz"* and of the *"toros ocultos"* of the torrid summer (*Noche del gran estío* and *El sediento*), of the *"toro estupefacto"* in the meridional *Ardor,* of the monstrous nocturnal bulls of fear.

Translated from the Spanish by BERNICE G. DUNCAN

Clamor I: Stylistic Peculiarities

by Concha Zardoya

Clamor WITH ITS THREE PARTS does not oppose *Cántico,* as the superficial reader might believe, but enlarges or opens its theme toward the history of man. If *Cántico* is "Praise of Living," *Clamor* is "Historical Time." If *Cántico* interprets the surrounding world—the unscathed world—as a function both of being and of astonishment of being, *Clamor* tends toward the revelation of man's living—a *"mundo herido,"*[1]—an intimate and dramatic experience, the collision of being with time. With *Cántico* and with *Clamor,* yes, Jorge Guillén affirms *"la hermosura de la vida sin exclusión de sus accidentes negativos y adversos, o mejor dicho, contando con ellos para mayor esclarecimiento"*[2] of total life—of that life that our poet proclaims *"más feroz*[3] *que toda muerte."*[4]

Cántico and *Clamor,* then, are complementary and never opposing books—books that, with *Homenaje,* constitute a trilogy that is a coherent whole, a unified work: *Aire Nuestro.* In it

---

[1] *"Sólo ese silbido/ Calma en la noche por un mundo herido"* (*Clamante, A la altura de las circunstancias,* 102).

[2] Fernando Quiñones, *"El último libro de Jorge Guillén"* (*Viviendo y otros poemas*), *Cuadernos Hispanoamericanos,* Vol. XXXV, No. 105 (1958), 346–48.

[3] Fernando Quiñones acutely observes that *"feroz"* here lacks any pejorative connotation, being an enthusiastic and joyful vital affirmation, as the rest of the poem corroborates (*Ibid.,* 347).

[4] *El acorde, Maremágnum,* 18.

themes, metrical forms, and stylistic modes are internally mingled, evidencing a continuity of life and creation: *"Continuidad poética de diferente calado, sin desfallecimiento y sin mácula."*[5] However different the styles of each part of the trilogy appear (Manuel Durán has already referred to *"las tres maneras de Guillén"*),[6] it seems to us that in each one, and therefore in all, the same intelligent and lucid vein of poetry is discovered, always elevated to a high category of artistic creation, always governed by a mind that selects, orders, disciplines, structures, and clarifies. Jorge Guillén, *"poeta radical,"*[7] requires as much of himself in *Clamor* and *Homenaje* as in *Cántico*. The former are not easier or more accessible than the latter. I do not mean to imply that there is in the three a certain kind of hermeticism or that one must possess a special key to understand them. There is as much poetic exigency in any stanza of *Cántico* as in a long poem of *Maremágnum,* the first book of *Clamor*. The same Castilian *señorío* exercises its asceticism of expression, more or less rigorous, according to the requirements of the theme of the book, without concessions in the three parts of this trilogy: control, contention, rigor, and poetic effectiveness. Perhaps in some poems a more moderate and constructed expression exists and, consequently, is more transparent. But in the rest, even in the most extensive, that watchful consciousness of the poet is always present: the transparency has been exchanged for density, intensity, and human profundity. As much poetic intelligence is in *Perfección* of *Cántico* as in *Potencia de Pérez,* a long poem from *Maremág-*

[5] E. A., *"Viviendo y otros poemas por Jorge Guillén,"* La Prensa, December 21, 1958.

[6] Manuel Durán, "Jorge Guillén: *Viviendo y otros poemas"* CCLC, (1959), 120.

[7] So called by Ramón de Garcíasol in "Jorge Guillén. *A la altura de las circunstancias,"* La Torre, Vol. XI, No. 44, (1963), 186.

num, even though the latter seems to be rhetoric or anathema. In both there exists an indivisible poetry that springs forth from a living vital man, Jorge Guillén, who is both poet and artist. In *Perfección* he is in ecstasy before the earth because his mind can understand it and his soul can love it; this comprehension and this love of the world make him feel free, fulfilled, happy, and at peace with himself and with others. In the second poem he suffers with men, besieged and mocked by the tyrant.

    Clamor, considered thus, is not very different from *Cántico,* which is precisely a poetic ordering of enthusiasm in the face of reality, in the face of the beauty of the earth. The difference is rooted in the fact that in *Clamor* realities—or rather, the forces that conspire against them—are other forces. Because they are different, they require, at least sometimes, other verse canons or other resources of expression, which are always controlled with the skill of a master, always transfigured by the genius of the poet. But at the bottom, or background, of *Clamor, Cántico* is always lying. Textual proof is found in a *trébol* entitled *Domingo* of *A la altura de las circunstancias:*

> Es el día del Señor,
> Suene música sagrada.
> Cántico sobre clamor.
>   —*A la altura,* 97

Jorge Guillén does not repent or deny what he has sung in his first book, and he will always return to it in search of peace or happiness during times of stress: he will sing again many more times. But in possession of a more humane wisdom, he admits in *Clamor,* especially in *Maremágnum,* the voices that his *Cántico* rejected: those of exile, grief, and contemporary agguish, with an exemplary, stoic serenity in many poems.

It has already been said that *Clamor "es el contrapeso espiritual a la actitud de Cántico: es la queja, el grito del vivir."*[8] We can even add that *Maremágnum,* above all, is a book that deals with the daily and the circumstantial in ways closer to the strident and the dissonant than to harmony, although the chord reverberates in the background or in a final hope. Daily experience, placed in historical context, is here valiantly revealed, even to scraping occasionally the edges of the anti-poetic, even to taking on a voluntary prosaic quality. It is a deliberate and conscious attitude. It is not so much a change of style or poetic philosophy as the strong desire to establish immutable evidence of an epoch in which it has been the poet's lot to live, a man among other men. All the cloudy, chaotic, indecisive aspects of the historic moment that Jorge Guillén totally eliminated in his *Cántico*—a gospel against nothingness—are shown in *Clamor* with the veracity of a historical document. The pressures that man suffers everywhere are evident here. The poet voluntarily departs from certain canons, from certain stimuli of complete perfection—never from all—to place himself at the level of the man in the street, to accuse, to reproach, or to scoff. The poet reveals his experiences and his conflicts, as a man of today, a historical man, a social man, but cloaks them with his humor or sarcasm. The *trébol* and the aphorism of old Spanish root have burst forth in *Maremágnum*. The song here turns into clamor and accusation in the presence of the frightful circumstances lived by man beginning with the Civil War in Spain and World War II. Although poems are not lacking that still radiate beauty achieved in content and form[9] (these are poems that directly connect the new book with

[8] Rogelio Barufaldi, "Jorge Guillén, *testimonio y esperanza,*" *CritBA,* Vol. XXXI, No. 1308 (1958), 370.

[9] But the latter seem more impassioned, closer to existence, to us.

the earlier one, whose essential meaning he does not repudiate in spite of everything, that even impose the law of harmony), the remaining ones, the most significant, reveal to us to what point the dark forces that govern men of today threaten life and fullness of being and beauty, *"la integridad del planeta"* of which Jorge Guillén sings in his celebrated poem.[10] Chaos reigns, the *maremágnum,* in the present time lived by everyone. Sorrow reigns. Nothingness exists or threatens.

Let us now enter *Maremágnum* and analyze its most dominant stylistic and metaphorical characteristics. With them and through them, the content and thematic structure of *Clamor* will become clear to us.

FIGURATIVE EXPRESSION

I. LOGICAL FIGURES

Jorge Guillén, a conscious poet and artist, shows in *Maremágnum* his ability to take advantage of logical figures, not to produce surprise or effect, nor simply as an artificial device, but to set forth more clearly the true, actual world and the persistence, underneath the chaos of the ultimate harmony, affirming the *"continuación de nuestro ser viviente"* (p. 16).

(1) *Antithesis.* It appears to be used with different purposes. Strictly, some poems and verses are constructed upon a conflict of ideas, feelings, and sensations. The entire book is based on the confrontation of order and chaos, life and death, love and hate, joy and sadness, beauty and ugliness, liberty and tyranny, government and anarchy, right and its abuse, harmony and dissonance, light and shadow, peace and war, truth and lie, the natural and the eccentric, the perfect and the imperfect, health and debility, hope and hopelessness, creation

[10] *Perfección, Cántico,* 240.

and destruction, reality and the material, the song and the clamor.

Let us look at several antitheses in the verses themselves. The first lines of *Potencia de Pérez* contain them: *"Hay ya tantos cadáveres/ Sepultos e insepultos"*; *"Hay tanta patria reformada en tumba/ Que puede proclamarse/ La Paz"* (p. 40). In fact the whole poem is only a series of antitheses expressed or understood: *"Cuanto más resplandece la Verdad,/Más difuntos la cantan,"* *"Donde hay Fe santamente se asesina"* (p. 42). The so much acclaimed, glorified, and anointed verse is *"Solo sobre su escena,/ Solo ante sus insignias y sus cruces"* (p. 50). It supports *"aquel Orden: su desorden"* (p. 52). *Luzbel desconcertado* is also a poem created upon and with antithesis: according to the angel of expiatory light, the world is *"Caos"* (p. 92), Creation has failed (p. 74), and the Earth is Hell (p. 75); the harmony of the Great Musician has failed (p. 74), since *maremágnum* reigns. Instead of the old God, Luzbel has invented the Critic, a goddess who moves *"un orbe portentoso,/ Más allá de los cúmulos unánimes"* (p. 82). *La hermosa y los excéntricos* is a long antithesis in which the opposite of Love is sodomy, called elegantly by the poet "eccentricity." The poem *Guerra en la paz* is a continuous antithesis, threatened by the *"Satán atómico"* (p. 164), the fatal *"cataclismo"* (p. 162).

(2) *Dialogism.* To give more force to the historical and psychological content of his *Maremágnum*, Jorge Guillén frequently uses dialogue. It forms part, naturally, of the prosopopoeia, of the metaphorical phenomenon of the humanization and personification in many cases. But, in the majority of the dialogues, it is Guillén's tendency to dramatize what he and everyone lives and feels—in this Time of History—which takes him to the use of this effective device. Thus, the poet creates a dialogue, although on some occasions it is tacit, and

he speaks with men, his poetical characters, the reader, himself, the bird at dawn, the mastodon, the flies, and even the motorcycle. Sometimes he makes his characters speak. Following the long monologue of Luzbel, the Governor and the Great Poet converse, and Pérez orders: *"Hombres buenos : creed, creed, creed"* (p. 47). This dialogism exercises its dramatic force in long poems, verses, and *tréboles* with questions and answers, interrogations and exclamations, and vocatives. It is tinged with seriousness, irony, or ridicule.

II. PATHETIC FIGURES

Jorge Guillén—moved by men's pain, disconcerted by the chaos that prevails in the world, angered by the subversion of values, affected by death and destruction, irritated by the discords and stridencies—breaks at some points the logical or rational discipline of certain verses, obeying inner forces and impulses, those of passion, anger, and sarcasm. These pathetic figures collaborate, as is natural, into that deep drama and human content that characterize *Maremágnum*. All of them, nevertheless, are restrained by the vigilant mind of the poet, always conscious of his task: the figures are employed and measured intelligently by the technical skill of the artist. They are never excessive in either disproportionate or hasty form: their repercussion is always balanced by the intense formal discipline that builds verses and strophes, although the long poems seem to have been created with the greatest freedom of expression. They are sparks of human life that transcend the form, breath, and human warmth, that surpass or renew the conventional expression, freed from all rhetorical ostentation. They are the trembling or outburst of the helpless or provoked creature facing the forces of evil that threaten life and beauty. They are just entreaty, they justly curse, they mask bitterness in sarcastic irony, or they even express the enthusiasm of the poet for the unextinguished beauty of the world and of some human beings.

(1) *The apostrophe.* (a) The poet curses with a simple exclamatory noun the very essence of what is cursed: *"¡Tirano!"* (p. 51). (b) He manifests censure: *"¡Vanidades, callad!"* (p. 67). (c) He expresses irony: *"¡Patria unánime!"* (p. 41), *"¡Júbilo de camisas!"* (p. 43). (d) He affirms his enthusiasm: *"¡Plenitud de hermosura en desnudez!"* (p. 67), *"¡Oleaje marino, feminino!"* (p. 63), *"¡Oh Capri de cristal en el calor ... !"* (p. 68), *"¡Ah, Reina de Naciones, mujer hermosamente destinada al hombre ... !"* (p. 143).

(2) *Epiphonema.* Many *tréboles,* verses, and long poems of *Maremágnum* finish with a final exclamation that intensifies its dramatic quality or its effectiveness: they are prolonged or resound in the mind of the reader. These exclamatory verses go beyond simple admiration because they are the final reflections pulled from our souls, suspended before the consideration of what has gone before. Because of this blending, they are converted into epiphonemas since they are conclusions of a foregoing exposition. In such epiphonemas Jorge Guillén often concentrates the most profound meaning of his strophe or his poem, being the subject and, likewise, the conclusions of them. Or irony, indignation, or sarcasm vibrate in them, pain cries out, joy sings: *"Trabajar es también sufrir. ¡Gran deber!"* (p. 39); *"Todo es bar y delicia oscura./¡Televisión!"* (p. 56); *"Nada es ahora más sabio,/Nada es más eterno. ¡Fiesta!"* (p. 196); *"Para el orbe no hay desengaños./¡Vida, vida: ved la segura!"* (p. 115).

(3) *The Exclamation.* Besides the apostrophes and epiphonemas, *Maremágnum* contains, on account of its explicit dramatic quality and its objective-subjective expression, abundant exclamations of all kinds: affirmative, ironical, sarcastic, and

condemnatory. These phrases appear in all kinds of poems, scattered but intervening always at the proper moment and in the right place. The extent varies and responds to the tensions of the poem. Sometimes the exclamation constitutes a *trébol*:

> ¡Y si este mundo no fuera
> Más que ese precipitado
> De realidad verdadera!
> —*M*, 102

At other times it may form half a strophe, as in *Luzbel desconcertado*, p. 81.

(4) *The Interrogation*. We decline to repeat here what we said with reference to the exclamation, but we have to add that some poems are formed entirely of various questions, like *Pared*, composed of six versicles and six questions. A single question gives body to certain *tréboles*. Many poems end with an anguished question to which the poet does not expect an answer. Sometimes the former is ironical or joking; at other times it implies reproach, stoic resignation, or universal acceptance; on occasion it is a riddle. But it never aspires in *Maremágnum* to the poetic ineffable: in this book, the sleepless man *"es la Pregunta"* (p. 24).

> Erudito: ¿por qué me explotas?
> ¿Mis cielos se encuentran abajo,
> Por esas nubes de notas?
> —*M*, 135

> ¿Qué señas nos esbozan esas nubes?
> ¿Se trata de vivir—o de morir?
> —*M*, 178

153

¿Es venenoso el mundo? ¿Quién culpable?
¿Culpa nuestra la Culpa?

—*M*, 17

Scattered through the poem, the questions create expectation, threat, anguish, and curiosity, as in *Guerra en la paz, Aire con época, Dolor tras dolor, Potencia de Pérez,* and *La hermosa y los excéntricos.*

METAPHORICAL PECULIARITIES

I. VIVIFICATION

Although humanization, dehumanization, *chosisme,* and degradation are the metaphorical peculiarities most abundant in *Maremágnum,* we have found two examples of vivification. In *Guerra en la paz* the word *"guerra"* with its strong *r*'s is vivified onomatopoetically in *"Mosquito monstruoso"* that buzzes, *"retorna y persiste"* (p. 161). In *Subida* the poet feels that the mountains are alive, like animals, on imagining that he walks joyfully through *"azuladas cumbres/ Con lomos siempre extraños a la Historia"* (p. 181).

II. HUMANIZATION

El acorde, a Heraclitean poem that serves as the introduction to *Clamor,* is the work in which Jorge Guillén affirms his faith in constant creation and in the triumph of harmony underneath all the discord. It begins with the humanization of the morning. The poet believes in it because each day discovers the world for him: *"La mañana ha cumplido su promesa"* (p. 15); yes, but *"duele"* and *"no se estrena"* because pain and nausea attack men. In another poem *"La tarde abruma a los ahora encorvados"* (p. 39) Andalusian workers. And because confusion reigns, *"La noche profundiza su propia soledad"* (p. 24).

Jorge Guillén, moreover, humanizes other forms of temporality in *Aire con época,* by means of humanizing adjectives, so that today triumphs over yesterday and the living prevail over the dead. But there is rubbish in the city, and the poet knows that *"el horror de la luz"* reigns over it, frightened by the *"hórridas ruinas"* (p. 54).

Jorge Guillén humanizes, then, the elements of nature. In a *trébol "el aire, tan cortés, ya es célebre"* (p. 100). In *El viento, el viento*—a poem that saves the beauty and the affirmation within *Maremágnum*—the wind, humanized, creates, speaks, suspects, sings, breaks forth, puts aside leaves and even sleep, and encircles and leads the poet but will not indulge his sadness. In *Viernes Santo, "la tierra se conmueve"* (p. 35). The sea takes human form in *Mar que está ahí:* it is a *"buen compañero, sencillo, cotidiano,"* *"infiel, caprichoso, perjuro"* (p. 171). In a *trébol* at break of day the poet proclaims the sun giver and ordainer of his life: *"Sea, sol, lo que tú me elijas"* (p. 96). The distances in our epoch between man and the stars are wiped out with an *"abrazo planetario"* since *"nada es ajeno al hombre"* and *"la luna está muy cerca"* (p. 176). Vineyards, given humanness, *"Recogen y cantan"* (p. 115) to the Wife after Love has been consummated. In a *décima,* a ten-line stanza, dominating with its song the multitude's shout in the square and in front of the shadow of Cortés, the birds of Cuernavaca are humanized as the *"últimos conquistadores"* (p. 125).

We also find in *Maremágnum* interesting humanizations of concrete things: the *"cristiano autobús"* (p. 97), *"cesante el farol"* (p. 100), *"estúpidos"* and *"soñolientos"* corners (p. 72); ruins are afraid *"con el temor de no ser ni su angustia"* (p. 54); the illustrious city *"aspira a ser perenne"* (p. 160) or *"erguida,/Duerme entre los insomnios"* (p. 25) of men or is a *"humilde proveedora fecunda"* (p. 154) of the sodomites.

The poet makes precise and concrete the imperceptibility and vagueness of the threat with humanizing verbs:

¿Se temerá a sí misma?
Y tiembla en el espacio matinal. . . .
—*M*, 160

¿La veis ahora? Tiembla. ¿No se atreve?
Se atreve, se desnuda,
A todos amenaza la Amenaza.

Flota, desciende, yerra,
Se fija en los vocablos. . . .
—*M*, 161

Jorge Guillén humanizes the abstract, in tragic parody, when he describes the *Potencia de Pérez*: *"La Verdad se desposa con el Régimen"* ...*"La Verdad avanza destruyendo"* (p. 42).

III. DEHUMANIZATION

This metaphorical process cannot be lacking in the chaotic world that Jorge Guillén denounces in *Maremágnum*. Man is degraded in it; he becomes an animal or is destroyed. The poor man, for example, is a *"gusano ya en andrajos con gusanos"* (p. 139). In the milieu of the eccentrics a forty-year-old woman displays a *"catadura equina"* (p. 145). The man who fled is an *"infeliz conejo"* (p. 48) and finally dies. To Lucifer men are *"desventuradas bestias—hombres/Y gallos"* (p. 72) who rest and crow. Pérez is an ex-man because *"se llama Pérez"* and because, above all, he is Pérez: the *"Pérez vergonzante" "el más terrible Pérez, que se llama Pérez y que lo es"* (p. 52). Pérez is a name—a man—depersonalized, without essence:

A solas silencioso el tan nombrado
No queda ni ante sí,
Figura sin figura
Si no se la proponen los espejos.
—*M*, 52

With this dehumanization, ironic and tragic at the same time, a maximum negation of being and of the man, Jorge Guillén submits the tyrant to the supreme catharsis possible in poetry; he depersonifies him as a *"fajín augusto"* (p. 47), and the soldiers who march before him also have ceased to be men, converted into a great "artifact," a *"máquina entre las máquinas mortí- feras"* (p. 51).

A dehumanization that exalts feminine beauty, by means of its vegetablization is seen in *La hermosa y los excéntricos:* *"¡Qué frutal por la piel, y con su riego de sangre-savia, tan animal y vegetal!"* (p. 140). The same type of vegetablizing dehumanization, applied to an eccentric, appears in the same poem: *"Hortensia escapada de su jardín, un adolescente ges- ticula, rápido, rítmico . . ."* (p. 142).

IV. DEPERSONALIZATION

We have already seen cases of "depersonalization" in the metaphor of "sash" applied to the tyrant Pérez and in "death-dealing machines" referring to the soldiers. *"¡Júbilo de camisas!"* (p. 43) contains an obvious example. In the long poem those that appear in the description of the parade sum it up, proving that those present are not persons but things: *"plumajes, char- oles, armas nítidas"* (p. 50). On the other hand, humanized are *"Las tribunas, repletas,/ Yerguen sus cortesías"* (p. 51). Pérez's ambient is absurdity.

For Lucifer the world was not created by God but by the

mind of man; it is a rocket, a thing, and a fleeting light (p. 82). For the poet, *"El mundo es un vagón, . . . Maremágnum veloz como un estruendo/ De tren"* (p. 30), and Europe is a sunken ship (p. 60). Jorge Guillén, finally, depersonalizes the abstract when he writes with pathos: *"No hay libertad, trasto viejo"* (p. 48).

V. CONCRETISM

Sometimes the poet tries to give flesh and blood, tangible and concrete reality, to something which does not have it. Thus, in the night, he tries to define the silence that surrounds him, conferring density upon it: *"Hay tal soledad de silencio/ Que me sume en sus espesores"* (p. 132). On the heights, he imagines for the wind merlons from which to contemplate and trace realities, to breathe deeply: *"almenado viento"* (p. 181). With this imagery he captures poetically the intangible and the invisible, suggesting height and rapture at the same time. In like manner he outlines mental work: *"Pero el magín es camino/ Que traspasa todo muro"* (p. 159). What is vast is made apprehensible by a metaphor that concretizes it, on detracting from it and limiting it, connoting more riches possessed: *"Con sosiego el mundo es palacio"* (p. 133). The abstract can likewise be materialized before the eyes of the imagination, creating a poetic super-reality upon the socio-ethical reality:

> No hay surtidor más alto
> Que la gran injusticia: funde estrellas,
> Apaga los destellos más felices.
> —M, 194

VI. DEGRADATION

The tyrant degrades the perfect geometrical forms, the

wise order of the world: again center of the disorder, god of a band that needs him:

> Ahí
> Céntrico ahí, perdura,
> ¡Cuántos le necesitan y le inventan!
> Que mande
> Sosteniendo aquel Orden: su desorden,
> Sus bandos,
> Sus chanchullos patrióticos.
>
> —*M, 52*

(Note how Pérez has displaced and inverted the centers, the focal realities, central in *Cántico.*) The sun, also, has demeaned itself by shining upon the false pomp that glorifies it, since it is *"tan cómplice"* (p. 50). The full noon that shines in *Cántico,* presides now over a dehumanized and false world: it is not the festival of Nature:

> El día redondea un sol muy rico
> De plumajes, charoles, armas rígidas.
> A tanta pompa en rigidez aplaca,
> Ya resplandor, el triunfo así arrojado
> Brillantemente a todos.
>
> —*M, 50*

The "rounding" does not refer here to the splendor of the sky at the central hour of the day, but hangs over the bull ring and the crowd, a soulless mass: *"Público en tarde redonda"* (p. 61). The perfect roundness has diminished with the rotation and the cruel contest. And the compact abundance that reigned in *Cántico*—"dense blue over the day" (*Perfección*)—is diminished in *Maremágnum* through representing in it a depopulated and

deserted world with cactus instead of plants—instead of the
central rose—submitted to the blind will of the chief:

> Pensamos todos a una
> Sobre un desierto compacto
> Para que a todos reúna
> Como emblema el puro cacto.
> —*M*, 48

The almost abstract lack of adornment that illuminates many
poems of *Cántico,* now, lessened or subverted, presides over
troubled negotiations (p. 42). Lines from *Coro de policía*
show that the *maremágnum* also has lessened and subverted
the joy of *Cántico,* since good fortune now consists in hunt-
ing man:

> Tal es nuestra dicha
> Que hasta el más honesto
> Desde alguna ficha
> Cae en nuestro cesto.
> —*Coro de policía*, 45

"Por ley de asesinato," tyranny reigns over the multitude with
"boca amordazada" (p. 53).

VII. SENSORY IMAGES AND METAPHORS

In *Maremágnum* sensations captured visually do not absolutely prevail, as they do in *Cántico,* because they are interwoven
with the aural in a like proportion: noise, uproar, and dissonance compose and condition the *maremágnum,* the historical
life. But let us examine first the chromatic texture of the book.

(1) *Chromatic variance.* If in *Cántico* Jorge Guillén raises
color to a plane of essential, elevated Parmenidean beauty, to

heighten with absolute clarity the pure, objective being, in *Maremágnum* he uses it to define ugly and beautiful realities that transpire in time, linking them to it in their historical becoming. At times he succeeds in employing it with a symbolical value; at other times, with psychological meaning. He intends to "paint" the epoch even when he does not force himself too much to load his palette with many colors: certain basic tints are sufficient for him to emphasize that which deserves to be underlined. The chromatic variation, in some cases, and the monochrome serve also for his purpose.

(a) *Colors in the yellow or warm series:*

White. Although not mentioned frequently, it is used in noun form or reinforced by an adjective. White is applied to women, Nature, the Andalusian houses, and, metaphorically, History: *"¡Aquel* blancor!" (p. 118) of the blond woman; *"Y jugando se asciende hasta las nieves/ De blancura feroz/ Sobre sus picos vírgenes"* (pp. 175-76); *"Sólo imperan muros de* cal" (p. 39); *"Diferir es manchar la gran* blancura/*De la Historia aclarada"* (p. 43).

Yellow. With this color and its variations—gold, ruddy, blond, and ocher—Jorge Guillén paints woman and gives color to the Satanic city. Thus, he colors entirely the verse *Pecas* and favors two adjectives and qualities that essentially possess it: dry leaves, autumn, sun, a woman's skin, wheat, and summer— establishing the differences that separate him from Mallarmé on contemplating the same reality. To the French poet it suggests signs of autumn, to Jorge Guillén, symbols of summer. Lucifer sees a city whose houses are lodgings of iniquity and have *"tejados viejos con tejas* ocres." (p. 75).

Red. Using red with yellow, Guillén colors two autumn landscapes, representing the trees that characterize New England and the exile's country, placing in counterpart his present

and his past: *"Arces* rojizos," *"un leve octubre* dorado *de chopos"*
(p. 179). With yellows and greens the red evokes the nocturnal
lights of San Francisco Bay (p. 126); with blue he vividly colors
the dress of a girl eccentric (p. 151). Red becomes dynamic and
even personified in the *muleta* and represents the bullfighter
who manipulates it (p. 61). Red lends its color to Good Friday:
"Es viernes hoy con sangre:/ Sangre *que a la verdad ya de-
semboca"* (p. 35). In *Potencia de Pérez* he anoints the tyrant
with blood and gives the most intense chromatic note, perhaps,
of the whole book: "Ensangrentado *Pérez bien ungido"* (p.
53). He characterizes signal lights by green, whose reality is
poeticized in: *"Los cruces en que el tiempo palpita,* verde y rojo"
(p. 133).

Green. The Spanish poet uses this color to paint landscapes,
the sea, and the *Jardín que fue de Carlota* in Mexico.

(b) *Colors of the bluish or cold series:*

Blue. He tints the grays of the waves of the sea. In the description of a hermaphrodite, he achieves a feminine air. In
Potencia de Pérez it is the color implied in *"¡Júbilo de camisas!"* (p. 43); upon a labyrinth of offices, he erects a future,
"azul *de estío* azul" (p. 43). Not once in the book appears the
glorious "dense blue" of *Cántico.* In *Maremágnum* blue, pre-
dominantly, is tinged with political symbolism or abnormality.

Gray. With black it is one of the most abundant colors in
the chaotic world denounced by Jorge Guillén in this work.
It is visible in the aluminum that *"refulgen como aceros"*
(p. 172) in *Tiempo de volar.* The Andalusian peasants are *"mo-
renos por herencia,* grises *en la luz, pálidos de fatiga"* (p. 39).
Europe, for the shipwrecked, the exile, becomes more and more
distant, enveloped more and more in gray mist (p. 60). Gray
are the walls—*"como láminas límpidas"* (p. 33)—of the modern city. The most intense and significant gray note appears

in *Guerra en la paz* evoking the landscape, the anti- or ex-landscape, invented by the atomic Satan: *"Duna de un mar ya seco/ Bajo un gris de abolidas calaveras"* (p. 164).

(c) *Luminous colors:*

Black. Many colors are dark, if not black, in *Maremágnum:* the theme requires it. Thus, the Gothic stones that appear in the square of *Guerra en la paz* are "grises o negruzcos" (p. 160). The brilliance of Lucifer defies the background *"tenebroso de penas/Humanas, humanísimas,/Sólo a nivel de* lúgubre *malvado,/ De tribunal terrestre"* (p. 90) and opposes the night of "hell," in which criminals delight. The human orb moves under a *"mediodía/De* sombras *condenadas"* (p. 82). Black is contained also in the anti- or ex-landscape created by the atomic bomb: *"Orilla con* espectros,/*Después difícilmente campo triste,/campo entre sus muñones,/Sus añicos* nocturnos,/*Su polvo"* (p. 164). Black lends an undefined, ambiguous color to the eccentrics' city landscape; *"Matrona ataviado de* oscuro" (p. 151). Finally, it is the color with which the poet alludes to the world of sleep: *"Quiero dormir y me inclino/Sin moverme hacia lo* oscuro" (p. 159).

(2) *Luminous sensations.*

(a) *The light:*

Nevertheless, light—triumphant in *Cántico*—reigns in the world of *Maremágnum.* Still the sun reigns in "Time of History," in spite of *"el día fosco"* (p. 16) prevailing; and, because it is so, *"llega a ser amargo"* (p. 16). Light, like life, goes on living *"bajo los cielos menos zarcos"* (p. 18). Light coexists, essentially, with the great harmony (p. 19). Dawns exist in *Tren con* sol *naciente* and in *Invasión.* Yet light is the divine eye of Creation in *La "U" maléfica* (p. 36). And still light reigns on the shore of *Mediterráneo,* where at midday the female body is offered in a rite *"al dios* solar" (p. 55). Furthermore, it rules on the Isle of Capri (p. 68). The sun also illuminates certain *tréboles,* verses, simple acts, and beautiful realities that still exist in the world. There is even moonlight. Lucifer himself is *"fatalmente el ángel/de la suprema* luz" (p. 73), *"de la luz ilimitada"* (p. 82), although his light neither guides him nor illumines him (p. 91). Light triumphs in the poem *Pentecostés* (perhaps inspired by the celebrated canvas of El Greco?). There are violent, symbolical lights in it, *"tumulto de* relampagueos," *"haces fogueantes," "cielo exaltado"* (p. 59). A tragic light also shines in *Maremágnum: "ciegos bajo su* luz"—that of Unreason (p. 189). The madmen are delirious; they despair before the inert world. The light, finally, hovers above the *Ruinas con miedo.*

(b) *The shadow:*

The shadow opposes the light. Jorge Guillén, in the chaotic world of his book, can contrast them and create haunting monochromes, dramatic atmospheres. He evokes the somber ambient of evil and destruction. He penetrates the shadows of chaos: *"Y el mal se profundiza,/Nos lo profundizamos,* sombra *agrega"* (p. 17). Lucifer will denounce *"la gran* tiniebla *del orden"* (p. 82), not being able to endure "la noche/*De ese 'infierno,'* su fondo/ Tenebroso *de penas/Humanas, humanísimas"* (p. 90). There is darkness in the dungeons, in the mines, in the assassination chambers. There is darkness in the foundations of the city, *"algo que escalofría"* (p. 191).

(c) *Chiaroscuro:*

Light and shadow oppose each other and contend, also, in *Maremágnum,* contrasting order and disorder, love and sorrow, beauty and corruption, life and death. The prison shadows contradict the light of noon (p. 82). The clamor of the suffering is made of *"rabia oscura o claridad rabiosa"* (p. 82). Jorge Guillén, nevertheless, knows how to create other surprising chiaroscuros, counterpointing inner realities and abstract concepts. The thinking of the insomniac, for example, is a "spark" that "luce *contra la* noche" (p. 24). In the abominable atmosphere of tyranny, of the peace that reigns over countless dead, the poet reflects: "*Cuanto más* resplandece *la Verdad,/Más* difuntos *la cantan*" (p. 42). The moral world also can create a chiaroscuro of ethical tolerance:

> ¿Que mi amigo es pecador?
> Así nos une la sombra
> De una claridad mayor.
> —*M,* 128

And the surrounding reality creates, in turn, very vivid chiaroscuros; in a town square full of light, for example, a Negro child jumps up and down in the light, without seeing "sombras *ni muros*" (p. 123).

(3) *Acoustical sensations.* The general titles of *Clamor* and of *Maremágnum* impose, within the ideological concept, an acoustical content that intensifies the total meaning of both works. It is not unusual, therefore, that the acoustical sensations —and the stylistic resources they require and develop—abound in the poems more directly connected with the theme or central themes. Auditory realities, stridencies, dissonances, shouts, groans, etc., permeate verses and strophes by means of nouns, adjectives, verbs, and adverbs, forming an acoustical texture of great power with which the "Time of History" evoked by the poet conforms. Under the dissonant and strident structure lies the agreement, the supreme aspiration to the final harmony.

(a) *Dissonant sensations*:

1. *Noun media:* shout, alarm, explosions, collision, eruption, traffic, clashes, chattering, ebullience, tumults, hubbub,

noise, howling, tri-motored plane, siren, cataclysm, double-beats, rupture, moan, etc.

2. *Adjective media*: brutal, torrential, rolling, discordant, groaning, clamoring, etc.

3. *Verb media:* bursts forth, to roar, to crunch, to grind, chirping, to bark, to split one's ears, to stun, to scream, to buzz, clamor, crush, unhinge, etc.

Examples: *"A borbotones/Se precipitan ruidos preñados de alborotos"* (p. 26); *"Ya el ruido/Del trimotor, costumbre discordante,/Forma una soledad de viento fiero"* (p. 172); *"Próximo pasa el tráfico rodante, La gran ciudad chirría, se apresura,/ Y sonando no deja de ofrecerse . . ."* (p. 160); *"Rumores de cadenas chirriando entre lados"* (p. 60). Finally, at the end of the confusion, in a remote zone, Harmony:

> . . . Y el tren, hacia su meta lanzándose, corriendo,
> —Mirad, escuchad bien—
> Acaba por fundirse en armonía,
> Por sumarse, puntual, sutil, exacto,
> Al ajuste de fuerzas imperiosas. . . .
>
> —M, 30

(b) *Melodic sensations:*

1. *Noun media*: agreement, concert, musician, singing, murmurs, birds, peals, clock, rhythm, song, music, harmony, whispers, cadence, choir of stars, rain, wave, range, lute, melody, counterpoint, silence.

2. *Adjective media:* sonorous, sounding, melodic, resonant, harmonious, vibrant, etc.

3. *Verb media:* sounds, to hum, to sing, resounds, modulates.

Examples: *"¡Cuántos pájaros en nido!/Música ya como ruido"* (p. 32); *"El pájaro solitario/Modula sus variaciones/ Para aliviar mi cansancio"* (p. 100).

(4) *Synesthesias.*

Jorge Guillén sometimes creates synesthesias by crisscrossing the perceptions of his senses, coloring them psychologically, or transferring to them, on an inner plane, the states of his mind— happiness, sorrow, irony, and sarcasm.

(a) *Sight-hearing:* "astros sonantes" (p. 147), "negros sonoros" (p. 33), "encendido fragor" (p. 58), "maná torrencial" (p. 59), "cumbre de sus voces" (p. 59).

(b) *Hearing-sight:* "orfeón de estrellas" (p. 93), "cadencia de aurora" (p. 65), "vibración de fuego" (p. 58), "golpes radiosos" (p. 59).

(c) *Sight-hearing-sight:* "claror que vibrase hacia la grana" (p. 116).

(d) *Sight-hearing-touch:* "Su forma, su vocablo,/Caliente y aún más allá del fuego" (p. 59).

(e) *Hearing-sight* (or *touch*): "Cantaba aquella piel" (p. 65).

(f) *Touch-sight:* "Era el blando relieve de las ostras" (p. 65).

(g) *Touch-hearing-sight:* "Me roza el ruido/Que la luz desencadena" (p. 159).

(h) *Transposed sensations:* "clamor con rabia oscura o claridad rabiosa" (p. 83), "amables murmullos espesos" (p. 126), "temblor incongruente" (p. 160), "fragor indignado" (p. 35).

Because it contains visual, olfactory, tactile, and gustatory sensations, we may consider that *La luna es una delicia* is a synesthetic verse. *Pentecostés* is the poem of words seen and colored; therefore, it also is synesthetic : *"Y el tumulto de luz fulgió con luces./Innumerables luces como lenguas/En vibración de fuego/Buscaban, descendían/Arrebatadamente . . ."* (p. 58).

FIGURES OF SPEECH

In studying the sensory content of *Maremágnum,* we have seen that there is an acoustical texture in it. The different resources of speech are summed up in it, fortifying its plot and its tone, its intensity and its loftiness.

(1) *Anaphora.* Jorge Guillén uses the anaphora not only as an element of melodic unity but as a thematic key of some poems and, moreover, of the whole book: the words *"maremágnum"* and *"clamor"* are repeated many times, along with *"acorde"* and *"armonía."* Others, also repeated, explain them in different degrees and variations. Such anaphoras, then, reinforce the unity of the work and interweave the central themes with their variants.

Some examples proving the richness of these anaphoras follow: *"acorde"* appears in the poem of the Introduction, *El acorde,* and begins the second part, *"Acorde primordial"* (p. 16); it reappears in the third strophe of the third part in developed form: *"El acorde a sí mismo no se engaña"* (p. 18). The anaphora is unfolded in the following strophe and frames two verses, as if the *acorde* might gain breadth: *"El gran acorde mantendrá en tu cima/ Propia luz esencial: así te asiste"* (p. 19). In the final strophe the accord reaches its plenitude on joining with the eternal starry concert. This progressive anaphora serves Jorge Guillén as a prologue and an epilogue to his book, fixing this idea in the mind of the reader; under the confusion of the world lies accord, harmony. Neither creation nor light ceases.

In *Mañana no será otro día* the anaphora *"de noche"* and *"el insomne"* appears alternately at the beginning of the lines, carrying our attention from one to the other, until finally the awakening is announced: the rebirth. The anaphora has marked the binary rhythm of the poem and, on disappearing, has mingled the night with the dawn: a resumption of life.

In *Tren con sol naciente,* *"vagón"* and *"tren"* appear in the first strophe and in the last two, in amplified form and with a new metaphor: the *vagón,* the real objective *tren*—in which the poet has been describing to us the passengers—has been converted into an image of the world: *"El mundo es un vagón."* *"Maremágnum veloz como un estruendo/de tren." "... Y el tren, hacia su meta, lanzándose, corriendo ..."* (p. 30). The anaphora has progressed and has fused with the poem of the Introduction; the roar of the train "ends by melting into harmony": the *acorde* has been achieved.

In *A pesar mío* we find a parenthetic anaphora (without variations), at the end of each versicle—*"(no lo entiendo)"*—to express the perplexity that dreams cause us; they are absurd because the realities dreamed about change, evade us, and are withdrawn from us.

In *Adoración de la criatura* the anaphora sets forth the subject of the poem, the girl Isabel, three times. In *... Que no* the anaphora is the ideological-thematic nucleus around which the poem turns. The "u" in *La "U" maléfica* is a vocal anaphora throughout the poem. In *Todos o casi todos los hombres,* the anaphora *"muerte"* appears at the end of the first and last strophe to counterbalance their meanings. Many anaphoras are scattered and interwoven in *Potencia de Pérez,* strongly connecting the tissue of the poem that, without them, perhaps would lose tension in its unity. The anaphoras link strophes together and effectuate meanings. They condemn the "protagonists" of the farce or the drama: *"Pérez"* and *"Jefe,"* his nickname, are each mentioned eight times. *"Orden"* and *"Verdad"* are mentioned four times, *"coro,"* six; and *"Dios,"* four. The word *"muertos"* appears on four occasions, and its variants also are mentioned: *"cadáveres," "difuntos," "sepultos o insepultos," "enterrados," "desenterrados."* In *Ruinas con miedo* the anaphora *"ruinas"* is presented in the title and in the last line, reinforced by its synonym variations *"escombros," "públicos esqueletos"* and *"paredes mutiladas."* In *Pentecostés* anaphoras also exist with scattered synonym variations: *"tormenta," "tumulto," "luces," "fuego," "encendido fragor," "relampagueos," "vibración de fuego," "cielo exaltado,"* and *"golpes radiosos."* In *Muchacha en Capri* the anaphora is the proper, geographical name given in the title, is repeated in an expletive exclamation, begins a line, and ends the last one in a double exclamation: *"¡Capri, Capri!"* (p. 69.) In *Luzbel desconcertado* there are many scattered anaphoras: the pronoun *"yo"* is repeated nine times; *"Dios,"* five; *"Él,"* two; *"el Otro,"* four; *"Ángel,"* four; and eight times the word *"clamor,"* against *"rezos," "quejas,"* and *"dengues venerandos."* It is obvious that the aforementioned anaphoras intensify the dramatic and conceptual force of the poem. In the same way they act throughout *Dolor tras dolor,* a poem in which this word is repeated on fifteen occasions, creating that atmosphere of tragedy which characterizes our period and thus marking one of the constant themes of *Maremágnum.* In *Guerra en la paz* the anaphoras create expectation and terror in that anguish over the atomic bomb and the war; this last word is repeated nine times and, together with it, *"amenaza," "cadáveres," "dolor,"* and *"clamor"* in some verses. In *La hermosa y los éxcentricos,* on the contrary, the anaphora serves to exalt the former under the synonym of *"Reina,"* which is repeated twenty-one times in various places; the anaphora points out in the book the triumph of beauty and chaste love over the dark passions of a promiscuous and negative world. Many other poems contain anaphoras that we cannot study here, but we are especially interested in mentioning *El viento, el viento* because it contains a type of anaphora that supports in a parallel or symmetrical form: the anaphorical title, duplicated in the first verse of the refrain (repeated twice) begins fourteen strophes of the poem. The first and the last form another refrain, but *"viento"* has been replaced by its synonym *"aires,"* the word that begins and ends these verses. (Let us take note that the anaphora here extols the wind, a theme very characteristic of *Cántico*.) Very few anaphoras appear either in the *tréboles,* on account of their brevity and conciseness, or in the *décimas.* We can say in conclusion that the anaphora abounds in the long, more extended poems, usually possesses a tragic or dramatic significance, and is used to revile, ridicule, extol, or, in some cases, express sarcasm.

(2) *Alliteration, onomatopoeia, and internal rhyme. Maremágnum* contains, as we have seen, a great variety of acoustical sensations and images, a great wealth of discords and stridencies, some harmonies and melodies, and rhythms of affirmative exaltation or passionate anger. The anaphora contributes enormously to the thematic structure and the understanding, by acoustical means, of many temporal realities. Alliteration, onomatopoeia, and internal rhyme combine to sum up this proceeding, increasing the effects of sonority or dissonance befitting the present world and the modern city.

Let us look at some examples.

(a) *Alliteration and onomatopoeia: "Rumor de transeúntes, de carruajes"* (p. 15), *"Al cómitre de antigua o nueva tralla"* (p. 18); *"A borbotones se precipitan ruidos preñados de alborotos"* (p. 26); *"Como un estruendo de tren./Y el tren hacia su meta lanzándose, corriendo"* (p. 30); *"En grises muros lisos con láminas límpidas,/vertical de un vigor sin vértigo suspenso"*

(p. 33); *"santamente se asesina"* (p. 42); *"Estrépito,/Contra-dicción, contraste"* (p. 82);

Correctos, brutales,
Sutiles, entramos,
Salimos, rivales
De lobos y gamos (p. 45).

Ay, la guerra . . . Zumbando,
Mosquito monstruoso,
Con un rigor de erre, erre, erre
"Guerra, guerra" va en alas,
Y retorna, persiste (p. 161).

Avispa—Vesubio—trompeta (p. 133).

Variando va la variante (p. 133).

¡U!
Esa 'u' de Belcebú . . . (p. 36).

(b) *Alliteration and internal rhyme*:

Y aparezca ese Pérez vergonzante
Que embrollo y perifollo casi ocultan:
Un Pérez, ay, terriblemente Pérez,
El más terrible Pérez . . . (p. 52).

La masa humana se apelmaza . . .
Con una amenaza de maza (p. 112).

Me crea lo que no era (p. 182).

El viento frente al poniente (p. 183).

Viento en este pensamiento (p. 183).

Clamante, suplicante (p. 187).

Que son los suburbios más turbios (p. 122).

Ganamos, gozamos, volamos (p. 56).

(c) *Cacophony:* In the "choruses" of *Potencia de Pérez* we note the ironic, ridiculing, and sarcastic function of the consonant rhyme and of the internal rhyme, producing cacophonic effects by means of consciously sought remainders:

> La ley levanta
> Frente al oficial cacumen
> La sacrosanta
> Letra que todos consumen.

> Cuando un jefe toca un timbre,
> Algo nuevo se enmaraña.
> Nadie rehuya la urdimbre
> De nuestra araña sin maña.
>   —*Coro de burocracia,* 44.

> Las llamas al hereje
> Le hacen señas: ven, ven.
> Dios es con Nos el eje,
>   Amén.
>   —*Coro de clerecía,* 49

(3) *Ellipsis:* His desire for concision and synthesis causes Jorge Guillén to utilize ellipsis in spite of the extent and pace

of many poems of *Maremágnum* (he had already done so in *Cántico*). Naturally, he does it more frequently in the poems that are traditional in form. The elision of the verb "to be" is the most common, although he also suppresses other verbs and other grammatical elements. Because of the ellipsis, sometimes the rhythm of the poem is changed since the clauses and phrases are abbreviated or shortened. The rapid rhythm can be altered, becoming slow and even syncopated.

Here are examples of ellipsis and, in some, we will observe a special dramatic quality, a noticeable intensity:

¿Es venenoso el mundo? ¿Quién, culpable?
¿Culpa nuestra la Culpa? (p. 17).

(Despertar: renacer) (p. 25).

Más justicia, desorden, caos viejo (p. 18).

Lloran las tres Marías. Hombre sacro.
La Cruz (p. 35).

Aplausos. Gritos. ¿Oreja? (p. 61).

Ocios, negocios, hasta luego,
Carreras de caballos, hola . . . (p. 108).

¿Libertad? ¿Y para qué? (p. 128).

Cadáveres, cadáveres, cadáveres (p. 163).

Conclusion

We have examined here certain logical metaphorical and stylistic "peculiarities" of *Maremágnum* and noticed that they are multiple and varied. We think we have brought significant motifs to the surface. Now we can conclude that they are encompassed in an eminently "orchestrated" technique—in spite of those "discords" and "antitheses" that we were mentioning —associated or coassociated intimately with the theme or themes of the work, with the Guillén vision of the world, with the human and creative personality of the poet, but embracing also a more ample technique: that of *Cántico* and that of *Clamor,* of which it is part. There are levels of meaning and traits of style that coincide in these books, so apparently different. Jorge Guillén, like any great poet, proceeds with the keen consciousness of the diverse and with the certainty that the diverse converges toward the total unity. The different meanings of the "particularities" always bring us back to an "ultimate sense" that constitutes the intimate unity of each work placed in the concrete totality of the subject-object. Whoever knows the complete work of Jorge Guillén will be able to recognize the synthesizing character of this convergence. The stylistic study of *Aire Nuestro* will reveal to us someday to what point and in what way *Cántico, Clamor,* and *Homenaje* are interrelated within a totally harmonious and coherent structure. The study of the themes not only will lead us to that keen comprehension of the whole, the global meaning of a unique work—really monumental— within the universal poetry of the twentieth century. We shall discover that its ultimate meaning is not tautological or doubtful but syncretic, multiple, shaded, rich, and profound, within a closely connected whole, within a balanced and harmonious structure. This study will permit us to enrich and enlarge our sentimental, spiritual, and intellectual contact with each one of its parts, inserted into a radiant totality.

The different techniques do not possess any virtue of their own but are, in fact, what ages most. What supports a technique, what gives rule to this body is a soul, a vigilant intelligence: it is a vision of the world and of man. Only that vision does not grow old; only it awakens in us and in the future reader the always-renascent emotion, eternally renewed and renewable. The "peculiarities" of a poet—that is, the very movement of his creative life—are not a simple addition, a factor that is added to the rest, the sum of an enumeration; they constitute the flesh, the living substance of his creative expression, and his message to mankind.

Within *Aire Nuestro*—total concept of the I, of things, space, time, life, and death, of being and of nothingness— *Maremágnum,* and along with it, *Clamor,* is as necessary and essential as *Cántico* and *Homenaje* because without it that total concept would not have been possible. Its objectivity is determined by the exterior world; this is not the beautiful and ordered cosmos of Nature, but the often chaotic social mechanism. *Maremágnum* precisely exposes and denounces it but also saves it for hope of an ultimate harmony in consonance with that of the universe.

Jorge Guillén— accused of human coldness, of historical extemporaneousness for his *Cántico* without historical thought, and of being pro-classic and possessing a pure expression—is elegant of voice (as if he were a minor poet instead of one of the greatest of Spain and the world) and affirms in *Maremágnum* his interest and his participation in the tragedy of present-day man, but without losing his faith in life as necessary salvation. He is involved with the historic life of his time since he succeeded in tearing off the masks of cultural reality and exposing the intrinsic stupidity and violence, the tragic defacing of human existence in the historical context of the twentieth century. There is, then, in *Maremágnum* an ethical-moral bond that links Jorge Guillén with the intense morality of the baroque poets, of Quevedo and Goya who also sensed the nocturnal and infernal abyss in Hispanic and world reality. On overcoming the disillusion—in so far as it refers to reality and the human condition—he is closer to Cervantes, also a positive writer who believed in the ultimate reality of virtue and in the positive force of existence.

The archetypal world of *Cántico,* elevated from life to essence, is complemented by the tremendous world of discord and stridency, the historical existence of man, that Jorge Guillén denounces in *Clamor* and in *Maremágnum,* particularly; the latter is a book full of annoying contradictions, tensions, uneasiness, and incoherence. *Maremágnum* is the confrontation of the poet with disorientation, evident insecurity, and terror of the world that surrounds us. His metaphorical, pictorial, and acoustical vision of the imbalance and the dissonances (we have already seen some aspects of his technique) that by his gibes and sarcasm could be unmasked is catalyzed and resolved in faith and hope, in vital affirmation, and in a final, Castilian, heroic, stoic serenity. What is corrosive, deforming, grotesque —gloomy men, silhouettes or shades of an Inferno—is dissolved in an aspiration toward light. *Maremágnum* is a judgment on the contemporary world—a form of catharsis—but it is not the Last Judgment. It is a document of national and universal history and an existential document of our century. It intrudes in the historical future without ceasing on this account to be united to *Cántico,* a super- or extra-historical book, affirming a profound continuity beneath the apparent thematic discontinuousness. On the other hand, *Cántico* and *Clamor* are joined genetically: when Jorge Guillén was writing the fourth *Cántico* he was already carrying *Clamor* in his mind, as Robert Weber has shown.[11] There are, then, no absolute frontiers between the two

[11] Robert J. Weber, *"De Cántico a Clamor," Revista Hispánica Moderna,* No. 2 (April, 1963), 109–19.

books. We have given some stylistic examples that, although they reveal changes and new meanings, also affirm an expressive insistence and continuity.

If in *Cántico* Jorge Guillén proclaimed—commenting on a verse by Juan Ramón Jiménez—that *"todas las rosas son la rosa,"* [12] does he not affirm in *Maremágnum* that "all Pérezes are the Pérez" of his book, that is to say, "all tyrants are that tyrant"? If this is so, it follows that in both books the absolute-universal is concretized and particularized in the same way. What has varied has been the object of the poetizing: the rose has yielded its place to the *"fajín augusto."* The affront, besides, overflows into affirmation because to hate evil is, simply, to exalt good.

In the face of the unscathed world of *Cántico,* of archetypal realities, *Maremágnum* is a dramatic-epic world with real persons, described with a technique that would be realistic if that super-real value of the universalizing symbol did not exist, since there are in it symbolical titles and personages. Again, reality is raised to the mode of *Cántico.* It was pure, yes, *"ma non troppo,"* in the words of its author. We could likewise say that *Maremágnum* is, indeed, a book of impure poetry, *"ma non troppo."*

Translated from the Spanish by BERNICE G. DUNCAN

[12] *La Florida, Cántico,* 352.

PERSONAL TRIBUTES
III

Jorge Guillén Came from Seville

by Vicente Aleixandre

I NEVER SAW JORGE GUILLÉN in Seville. The first time I heard of Jorge was when I had already completed my studies and he was applying for a teaching position. But consistently I heard of the poet when he was already residing in the city of Murcia; he was a professor at the university there. Together with Juan Guerrero Ruiz, upon whom Federico[1] playfully conferred the title of Consul General of Poetry, he published in the Levantine city that unforgettable youthful literary review called *Verso y Prosa*.

In the aura of this generation there are four conspicuous reviews, it seems to me, that grouped our poets and brought them to light: two Andalusian, *Litoral* and *Mediodía*; one Levantine, *Verso y Prosa;* and another Cantabrian, *Carmen*. These were the four principal and direct sources, although the voice could be heard and spray burst forth through other channels as well.

I do not know what Jorge Guillén owes to Murcia. I do know that when I saw him most often—we were in Madrid— he was already a professor of literature in Seville. But he came to Murcia, alighting for a few quiet moments among his friends and companions, difficult in his elegance, almost cutting in his acuteness, ascending in his livelinesss. The professor from the

[1] Federico García Lorca.

shore of the Guadalquivir, oblivious to lecture hall and lecture, arrived fortuitously from the real Seville, and when I saw him it seemed to me that he could not have come from anywhere but brilliant Seville. There was in Jorge a thread of transparency that was not Murcian in any way but could have been at home, warmly received and even defined and contagious, in the southern ambience of Seville. Erect and self-contained, alive, he could be like the Giralda, and not in vain did another poet-companion exalt it as "a tower of taut wires." That "tower" is symbolic of Jorge, rising into the air of Seville, so very Guillén-like, touching its sharpness until he catches fire in that inspired and sparkling light from which he rightfully comes to us.

Later indeed, coming from Seville, a Castilian who had passed through Seville, unlike Andalusians passing through Castile, Jorge increased his own light, perhaps by giving it a touch of sensuality, making it more substantial and worthy of adoration, with that fire that reaches its zenith in transparency and lends it its combustion, its ultimate point of love and revelation.

> Funden lo vivo y lo puro:
> las salas de este jardín.

A Sevillian still, as much as the lightning that crosses the city, Jorge came from there, recondite and very clear, doubting and certain, with the enigma of his knowledge and in full possession of all that happened to him. Through Seville he passed, and there he remains. Jorge passed through that air and mysteriously arrived unchanged, yet different, among us.

Translated from the Spanish by BERNICE G. DUNCAN

Living with the Poetry of Jorge Guillén

by Dámaso Alonso

Years pass, many years, and we realize that this lapse of time was necessary for us to come to understand many new things that saw the light in our youth, that we considered ours with that selfishness of youth that always thinks itself master of its time, its epoch, and its "things."

It has been my lot to see many marvels, and not only to see them come into being but to be very close to the point where they were being born, opening up, or arising. One of these marvels, which a series of circumstances or necessities brought very close to me, was the poetry of Jorge Guillén.

Our generation was passionately devoted to modernism (not all generations are zealous to this degree). What was modern could be the theme, as in the poetry of Salinas or Alberti; at other times, the modernism consisted precisely in an unusual way of saying things. The latter is what many of us then considered the primary value of Guillén's poetry.

I recall the timid enthusiasm with which I attended the reading of Guillén's poems at one of those infrequent soirées in Seville which were our public debuts. I feared that they would fall into a chilly lack of comprehension on the part of the scanty audience (the night of my reading the only four ladies who were in the room had gotten up and made for the door—

single file—taking advantage of my drinking a glass of water).
I was there on the platform while Jorge was reading, so fear-
ful that I even tried to force applause in a no doubt badly
chosen moment. But the president, Sr. Garzón, made a tact-
ful gesture so that I would not go on with it. No, it was not
going to be necessary. Jorge had selected his poems very discreetly (like food for juvenile stomachs), and he read very well
the one:

> que toda la noche brilla
> con calentura amarilla
> ¡ay, amarilla, amarilla!
> ¡ay, amarilla, amarilla!

The audience, without stopping to inquire why the night
was shining with a yellow warmth, was already a part of them
(the night and the warmth) and applauded with great enthusiasm, because wherever there is poetry, there must be communication of an affirmation, in spite of the senses, in spite of
reason.

The public applauded, and I breathed easy. The fact was
that I knew (I was one of the few who knew, so I thought
then) that I had there, at my side, something new—the poetry
of Jorge Guillén—that by its clean, hard newness was difficult
to communicate to a public still preoccupied with pale, sad
princesses.

The recognition of something new, of birth of a new poetry
was almost our secret. There was a certain distrust in the face
of the great vacuum, the great *nada,* or the absolute zero that
surrounded us; but, at the same time, there was a certain pride
in knowing that we were isolated, united by the isolation, committed to mutual defense against the common danger.

Many years have passed and now I realize how incomplete was the knowledge we had of the poetry of Jorge Guillén. It had to develop throughout a life, and our life equally had to mature. Understanding is never illumination at a given moment, sudden and total. It needs time to grow, and life, too. I think that even those of us who saw it born at close range have only now come to understand much better the abundance of its values, its newness, its profundity, its extraordinary fertility of themes, its aspirations, its emotions, its penetration of our life and our epoch.

Translated from the Spanish by Bernice G. Duncan

A Half-Century of Friendship

by Jean Cassou

A half-century of friendship with Jorge Guillén is a half-century of friendship with the harshest and most stripped-down utterance of the Spanish genius; with Zurbarán, Cotán, Juan Gris, Góngora. Those Spaniards know nothing but manifest things—things that they handle, juxtapose, confront, or arrange somehow in equations: by this their evidence and substance are reaffirmed. Sometimes this affirmation is founded on the contrast and the difference with the nearest of other things. Sometimes it is made through a surprising analogy with whatever trait, whatever quality, whatever function, of another thing extremely far removed. But in every way and according to all the possible combinations of such a presentation, the entire universe enters into the presentation, decomposes there, is recomposed there, is summed up there.

Presentation. Affirmation, evidence of a presence. Of a present. No shadow, if not outside this present and to emphasize its outline. But no shadow can be introduced into the present or blend with it, no chiaroscuro can cloud it. Shadow relieves only the past and the future. Our memories are lost in darkness, our aspirations and presentiments venture into another darkness, that of the unknown. But the present stands in full light. All is present with these Spanish geometricians whom we have named above, who are the best of Spanish expression, of Spanish statement and viewpoint. Like them, Jorge Guillén speaks and sees. He declares. He makes clear. He presents in open clarity that which is. He indicates it. He indicates a presence in his present. The presence is in the present indicative.

It is in the present indicative that Jorge Guillén's expression is conjugated. All of his "canticle" is in the indicative mood, of the present tense, in the present indicative. And the universe would not know how to sing his song in another tense or another mood. The poet's whole existence has been consecrated to this universal canticle which knew neither past nor future, but present, stubborn present, present presence. The entire universe, we said, had entered into this canticle conjugated exclusively in the present: hence the temporal universe with its past and its future, these compressed, flattened into the sheet of this present; and also the spatial universe—space, lands, seas, stars of the firmament, places; now, places exist so that things may happen there, but in these nothing happens. Nothing happens, since the instant alone exists: hence the places are reduced to one single place which is the place of the instant. Perhaps, a metaphysician would call this prodigious reduction eternity. But that is only a word, and, contrary to the metaphysicians, poets are not at all satisfied with a word: actually, they have all words at their disposition. If they manage to accomplish a reducing operation, it cannot be put into a formula at all but is manifested in action, in the operative action that uses all words, all, absolutely all, and in senses and positions of such diversity that they seem to pass beyond the number of all words as the dictionary counts them and to add new ones to them.

So the art of Guillén is a synthesis which does not tell its name, an operation that reduces the universe to a single present moment; but this operation is not translated into a systematic and conceptual language. This rule of using only the present indicative is not enforced anywhere; it marks only the manner, the compartment of poetry; it establishes the rule, but it never appears as a constraint. This poetry feels at ease and is happy to be in the present indicative. It rejoices in it, reaches joy through it. What is a canticle if not a joyous outpouring of the present? The soul is unhappy in the past. In the future it is uncertain and hesitant. The past it regrets. In the future it feels lost. But the soul conjugated in the present indicative is at the highest degree of simplicity and gladness, like a piece of music in C major.

In this tonality Jorge Guillén's poetry is saturated with being and the wish to be. And being is the supreme perfection, according to the theologians who, with their famous ontological argument, make being itself the proof of being. Let us leave the theologians there, as we have left the metaphysicians, for nothing matters here but poetry, which neither proves nor seeks to prove anything. Being does not prove itself but is satisfied to show itself. Guillén's poetry shows being, does nothing but show it, and shows nothing else. And what splendor in this showing forth/*monstrance!* What gold has gone into it, what fires it flashes outward, what a fascination it exerts on the eyes of those who behold it and who are persuaded of the holy nature of the presence it contains! But this holiness is none other than that of the universe, the whole of it concentrated in his awareness of living.

It is this immanence that here makes the law. There is no departing from it. If any exclamation explodes in Guillén's poetry, it is by no means in the vocative. It is not at all the way resorted to by all other lyric poets, in a solicitation which ordinarily invokes, evokes, adores, pleads, defies, or inveighs. In short, it is not something toward which there is motion and from which, in return, an answer is expected. With Guillén the exclamation does not go toward anything else whatever and would not know how to be anything but the reinforcement of the designated presence and, in grammatical language, an apposition to this term—an apposition which takes the tone of jubilation. For it is not enough merely to assert being: it is further necessary, to this assertion, to add wonder. When the assertion is communicated, when it is proclaimed before the eyes of the spectators, they are forced to go along with this mad, paradoxical statement that being is not enough, for there must be also the resplendence of being.

Guillén's poetry is therefore tightened to excess, but from within and in its own immanence, which is immanence to the universe. It is, in this immanence, a fulfillment. It fulfills itself, only through itself and only in itself. It is what has been called perhaps, in a certain period, pure poetry. It must not be understood in the sense of excluding what is real and human. Let us repeat: it is universal life, hence the reality itself manifested in the poetry of Jorge Guillén. And after long years occupied with the growth of the sublime *Cántico*, other collections were born, where this reality of the universe is revealed as more direct, moving, tragic, and human. Guillén's poetry is in the present but the world we live in and the times we live in are also in the present, and this present is dramatic, sometimes to the point of agony. This, Guillén has never forgotten, and why would he not say it, why not give it expression? No matter what the new cares, the new turns the years may give to the poetry of Guillén, we will always find there once more the imperious presence of the present. And always it will have occasion to declare the inexhaustible richness of the present. But how could it be otherwise with a poet who has accomplished this herculean exploit of forcing all the indeterminable multiplicity of the world to be contained in the present?

After half a century it is in the present that I see my friend Jorge. I have never known anyone who, more than he, gives the impression of finding himself satisfied to be in the present minute, to feel himself there, to expand there, perpetually curious and amused by the events of the present minute, perpetually exalted by its animation. The half-century can pass: I find him the same—unchanged, slim, dry, agile, lively, a pure Castilian of Old Castile. He is an unalterable Castilian, stripped of everything superfluous, like a root that roots him in Valladolid, capital city, capital par excellence, where the purest Castilian is spoken with the purest accent, and he himself, Jorge Guillén, speaking without pause, for that is his exclusive and jealous vocation: to give expression. Actual expression, present expression, to be a present that expresses itself. All of his life, which is connected with the universal life, flows into this wingèd word, tumultuous, droll, the glance and the smile which light up the lens of the glasses, and all joined in a crystalline effusion which does not spill out but stays in one place, being an effusion of the moment only. Nothing before, nothing after, nothing outside—nothing useless. Also, one understands all the stoic fortitude there is in the manner in which this Castilian, this lump of Castilian rock, of Castilian diamond, has accepted exile. One day, against the background of the gracious and generous university in the United States where he was teaching, some American ladies asked him amiably: "Surely you are going to return to Spain one of these days?" "No, never," he replied. "But why?" "Because I am a Spaniard." It would be hard to know how to affirm more proudly, or with a finer grace and serenity, this inflexible quality of being, which is Guillén's principal faculty. He is what he is, where he is, wherever his destiny—identified with his honor—places him; but he *is* this being as strongly and intensely as possible. And this cannot but be accompanied by that formidable happiness of which we have spoken.

The happiness of being appears throughout the career of this exemplary poet: in his attachments and affections, in all the elegance, strict and, as it were, miraculously easy, of his behavior. And so in his handwriting. There are handwritings, for example of certain men of action, that are dynamic and rush to the attack. Those of others, poets, have none of this violence of movement at all. Nevertheless, they go forward; only they do it rhythmically, harmoniously and in the manner of a melody—a melody which may be slow, nay refined and rounded, but which, in the end, is unrolled on the page, hence in time and space. Still other handwritings, also of poets, are black, supported by a fine, vigorous plasticity, extremely energetic, hence in motion also. The writing of Jorge Guillén, on the contrary, does not progress (belonging to a man of the present), but develops in place, vertically, in floral forms. The letters that compose it are likewise of the present; they stretch, tie and untie their charm where they are, after the fashion of plants whose flexibility is exercised only upward from the soil that holds them.

Translated from the French by CONSTANCE WAGNER

Jorge Guillén

by SALVADOR DE MADARIAGA

AT THE END OF AN ESSAY, published a few years ago, dealing with Vergil's influence on Spanish letters, I was bold enough to proclaim Guillén the greatest living poet of Spain. He soon wrote to me with a characteristic blend of modesty and wit, proclaiming himself the greatest poet of Valladolid.

I recall this episode because it enables me to redress a wrong. I do believe that I then overlooked Rafael Alberti, whom I should rank neither above nor below Jorge Guillén. Alberti does not come from Valladolid, a fact which endows him with some gifts while depriving him of others. Whenever he gets lost in his ideological north-northwest, Alberti topples lamentably down the crevasse toward—no, not craziness but something worse which I shall not describe more accurately out of respect and admiration for his poetry.

When he lets himself live away from his dangerous sector, Alberti is a marvelous poet, a kind of marvel Valladolid does not give forth, for it springs from the Andalusian gift of mother wit—a gift, by the way, not every Andalusian finds in his cradle. Cernuda, for instance, great poet though he was, did not tread that way and, as a poet, he might have been born in Castile or in Leon or in that Leon-Castile which is Valladolid.

The marvel of Andalusia is fantasy. Something beyond imagination, or at least different from it. The way of imagination, one travels toward a deeper realism; the way of fantasy, one wanders toward a wider realism, an extra-realism, a variation on the theme of the world. Imagination leads to Cervantes and Goya; fantasy to Góngora and Picasso.

But Guillén comes from Valladolid. He was born in a land where gifts are balanced. The lyrical trend of Galicia-Portugal is there tempered by the plastic sense of Valencia-Catalonia and tightened by the dramatic spring of Castile-Basqueland. Guillén is then an intra-realist, an essentialist. He penetrates inside reality in order to express what reality conceals under its appearances. He penetrates into things by the way of imagination, but before the temptations of fantasy, he stands in a kind of reserve. In him, as in Antonio Machado, we observe an attitude of "up to here but no further" which is the deepest feature of this kind of Spaniard.

Sobriety. More of the owl than of the goldfinch. More sententious than eloquent. A glance as sharp as the Andalusian's; but, if in the case of the poet of El Puerto, his eyes, drunk with light, make fantasy boil up into a profusion of verbal felicities (*La plaza de toros* of Alberti) in the poet of Valladolid, his penetrating eyes project the profile of things on the verbal scheme with a geometrical exactitude (*Mesa y sobremesa* of Guillén).

All this leads to an easier universality for the Castilian than for the Andalusian. The Andalusian can but with difficulty pass the Pyrenees. I very much doubt that Lorca could have attained his round-the-world fame had not his life been cut short by the tragedy that made us all the poorer. A Chinese journalist once asked me: "But, really, would you think Guillén as big a poet as Lorca?" and I, in my turn, asked myself in silence: What can this countryman of Confucius make of *"noche que noche nochera"*? The best of Lorca, just as the best of Alberti, bears no translation. The best of Guillén does. That which in Lorca or in Alberti turns out to be untranslatable is not merely due to the language but to the substance (thought, feeling, attitude, mood, fantasy, grace, gesture—what you will). Guillén is universal in both form and substance. (This is no award, no preference, but a mere distinction.) Guillén is a kind of Spanish Paul Valéry. But do not make me say that he imitates or follows Valéry. Both are springs of intellectual love rising toward the sky, parallel but different. And, in my view, if one of the two rises higher than the other . . . well, let's not complicate matters.

POEMS IN HOMAGE
IV

Estrofa

A Jorge Guillén

De tanta primavera oscurecida,
de tanta voz que se tragó la mar,
tanta preciosa sangre, tanta herida,
tanto lento morir, tanto llorar,
queda aún en la cima de tu vida
ese arrebol que nunca el viento ha de apagar

Rafael Alberti

Roma, 1967.

Estrofa

A Jorge Guillén

by Rafael Alberti

De tanta primavera oscurecida,
de tanta voz que se tragó la mar,
tanta preciosa sangre, tanta herida,
tanto lento morir, tanto llorar,
queda aún en la cima de tu vida
ese arrebol que nunca el viento ha de apagar.

El Poema: Homenaje a Jorge Guillén

by Carlos Bousoño

I

Dejad que la palabra haga su presa lóbrega,
se encarnice en la horrenda miseria
primaveral, hoce el destino, cual negra teología
corrupta.
       Súbitas, algunas formas
mortales, dentro del soplo de aire
permanente e invicto.
La palabra del hombre, honradamente
pronunciada, es hermosa, aunque oscura,
es clara, aunque aprisione
el terror venidero.
Hagamos entre todos la palabra
grácil y fugitiva que salve el desconsuelo.
. . . Como burbuja leve, la palabra
se alza en la noche, y permanece
cual una estrella fija entre las sombras.

2

Y así fue la palabra
ligero soplo de aire
detenido en el viento,
en el espanto,
entre la movediza realidad y el río

de las sombras. Ahí está detenida
la palabra vivaz, salvado este momento
único
entre las dos historias.
. . . De pronto el caminar fue duradero
y el hombre inmortal fue,
y las bocas que juntas estuvieron
juntas están por siempre.
Y el árbol se detuvo en su verdor
extraño, y la queja
ardió como una zarza
misteriosa.

3

Allí estamos nosotros.
Allí dentro del hálito.
Tú que me lees estás allí
con un libro en la mano.
Y yo también estoy.
Tú de niño, cual hombre, como anciano,
estás allí.
Tu corazón está con su amargura,
ennoblecido y muerto.
Y vivo estás.
Y hermoso estás.
        Y lúcido.

4

Todo se mueve alrededor de tí.
Cruje el armario de nogal, salpica
el surtidor del jardín.
Un niño corre tras una mariposa.
Adolescente, das tu primer beso

a una muchacha que huye.
Y huyendo así, huye nada
quieto en el soplo tenue.

5

Y así fue la palabra entre los hombres
silenciosa, en el ruido
miserable
y la pena,
arca donde está el viento detenido
y suelto,
acorde suspendido y desatado,
leve son que se escucha
como más que silencio, en el reposo
de la luz, de la sombra.
Así fue la palabra,
así fue y así sea
donde el hombre respira,
porque respire el hombre.

Homenaje a Jorge Guillén

by MANUEL DURÁN

Líneas, luces, blancura: lo profundo se aclara,
los ojos lo reflejan, y esas cúpulas grises
se resuelven en nubes, en silencio que flota.
Al fondo las colinas, diminutas y exactas.
La mirada construye sus puentes incesantes.
Dos caballos disparan sobre el azul intacto
sus crines y sus patas como flechas de pluma.

¿Es el mundo del sabio? Lo es más bien del amante,
de aquel que con sus labios, con su encendido abrazo,
recoge la belleza, la conserva, la exalta.
Y lejos, sensitivos, los álamos conmueven
el aire con sus hojas, con sus nerviosos verdes.
El mundo no es perfecto, pero existe y es nuestro,
y las voces oscuras, los gritos, los disparos
no harán que sus amantes cesen en sus abrazos,
en sus sabias caricias, como el álamo verde
que se abraza a la brisa, y la brisa al espacio;
y nosotros vivimos; el mundo es verdadero,
el combate no cesa; la luz está cantando.

Homage to Jorge Guillén

by Manuel Durán

Lines, lights, candescence: the depths are clearing,
his eyes reflect it, and those gray domes
dissolve in clouds, in floating silence.
In the distance the hills, diminished and precise.
The gaze lays down its endless bridges.
Two horses dart over unshattered blue
their manes and fetlocks like feathered arrows.

Is it the world of the sage? Rather the lover's,
who with his lips, with embrace afire,
possesses beauty, preserves, exalts it.
And distant, responsive, the aspens stir
the air with their leaves, with their tremulous greens.
The world's not perfect yet, exists though and is ours,
and no dark voices, cries, explosions
will sway its lovers from their embracing,
with their sage caresses, as the green aspen
clasps the breeze, and breeze the universe;
and we live: the world is real,
the struggle does not cease; the light is singing.

Translated by Katharine Meech

A Jorge Guillén

by Jaime Ferrán

No hubiéramos venido
si no fuera la tuya
una generación
    que nos dió aliento,
        en tiempo
de incertidumbre,
    si no fuera
porque nos enseñaste claridad
aunque no nos gustara.

No hubiéramos sabido
venir,
  si no es para decirte estas palabras
que hemos ido escribiendo,
       sin saberlo,
durante todos estos años.

      Fuiste
como un viento civil en nuestra vida
—Aire nuestro—
     de todos
los instantes de duda,
      cuando tú,
        desde lejos,
sin saberlo también,
     marcabas el camino.

Nadie pudo
repetir la justeza
de tu ademán,
                    Mas siempre
lo tuvimos presente.

No debe molestarte
que hayamos sido díscolos.

                    Teníamos
tan pocas rebeldías
a nuestro alcance,
                    cuando comenzábamos.

Pero estamos aquí,
                    queríamos decírtelo
y ahora que es la hora
                    nos faltan las palabras.

                    10 Febrero, 1968
                    En vuelo de Syracuse a Oklahoma

To Jorge Guillén

by JAIME FERRÁN

We would not have come
if yours weren't
a generation
        that gave us spirit
                in a time
of uncertainty,
        if it weren't
that you taught us clarity
though we might not like it.

We would not have known how
to come,
      if not to say to you these words
we've been writing,
           without knowing it,
for all these years.

          You were
a civilizing current through our lives
—Aire nuestro—
        of all
the instants of doubt,
        when you,
           from afar,
also without knowing it,
        were marking the road.

No one could
match the rightness
of your gesture.
                    But always
we had it in mind.

It should not disturb you
that we may have been wayward.

                    We had

so few causes
within our range,
                    when we began.

But we are here,
                    we wanted to tell you all this
and now, that it is time
                    words fail us.

                    February 10, 1968
                    En route from Syracuse to Oklahoma

          Translated by KATHARINE MEECH

APPENDIX

Jorge Guillén: A Biographical Sketch

Jorge Guillén born January 18, 1893, Valladolid, calle de Caldereros (today Montero Calvo) 11.

Family

Father: Julio Guillén Sáenz, Valladolid, 1867–1950.
Mother: Esperanza Alvarez Guerra, Valladolid, 1869–1923.
Elder brother of Julio (died 1933), José Jesús, and María.
Married in Paris October 17, 1921, to Germaine Cahen, 1897–1947.
Children: Teresa (now Mrs. Stephen Gilman), 1922 in Paris. Claudio, 1924 in Paris.
Second marriage in Bogotá, Colombia, October 11, 1961, to Irene Mochi Sismondi.

Studies

Childhood teacher: don Valentín Alonso. (The *"santo franciscano"* of the poem *Aquellas ropas chapadas* in . . . *Que van a dar en la mar.*)
Bachillerato from the Institute of Valladolid. (The first four years in San Gregorio.)
Student of Philosophy and Letters, University of Madrid, 1911–13 (Resident of the "Residencia de Estudiantes.")
Licenciatura en Letras, University of Granada, 1913.
Doctor of Letters, University of Madrid, 1924.

Academic Career

Lecturer in Spanish at the Sorbonne, 1917–23.

Examinations for professorship in Spanish Language and Literature, Madrid, 1925.

Professor at the University of Murcia, 1926–29.

Lecturer in Spanish at Oxford University, 1929–31.

Professor at the University of Seville, 1931–38.

(September, 1936. Jailed in Pamplona. *"Inhabilitado para cargos directivos y de confianza,"* 1937. Voluntary exile since 1938.)

Professor at Middlebury College, 1938; at McGill University, Montreal, 1939–40.

Professor at Wellesley College, 1940–57. Professor Emeritus, 1958.

Visiting Professor at Yale University, 1947; at the Colegio de México, Mexico City, 1950; at the University of California, Berkeley, 1951; at Ohio State University, Columbus, 1952–53.

Charles Eliot Norton Professor of Poetry at Harvard University, 1957–58.

Visiting Professor at the University of the Andes, Bogotá, 1961; at the University of Puerto Rico, 1962 and 1964; at the University of Pittsburgh, 1966; at the University of California, San Diego/ La Jolla, 1968.

Awards

1955 Award of Merit of the American Academy of Arts and Letters, New York.

1957 Poetry Prize of the City of Florence.

1959 Etna-Taormina Poetry Prize, Sicily.

1961 Grand Prix International de Poésie, V Biennale de Knokke-Le Zoute, Belgium.

1964 San Luca Prize, Florence.

Travel and residence abroad

October, 1909–February, 1911, in Fribourg, Switzerland, at the Maison Perreyve of the French Fathers of the Oratory.

1913–14 in Halle and Munich, Germany.

Since 1917 frequent residence in France.

1929–31 in England.

May, 1934 Lecturing in Romania.

Since 1938 in America. (Canada, the United States, Mexico, Colombia, Ecuador, Peru.)

1958 in Greece. 1962 in Belgium and Portugal. 1964 in Holland.

1910, 1934, 1951, 1954, 1955 in Italy with frequent visits since 1958.

Present residence: 15 Gray Gardens West, Cambridge, Massachusetts.

A Jorge Guillén Bibliography

a. Poetry

1. *Cántico*. Revista de Occidente. Madrid, 1928. 171 pp.
1a. *Cántico*. "Chefs-D'Oeuvre des Lettres Hispaniques." Centre de Recherches de l'Institut d' Études Hispaniques. Paris, 1962. 101 pp.
   (Reprint of the 1928 edition.)
2. *Cántico*. Second enlarged edition. Cruz y Raya. Madrid, 1936. 306 pp.
3. *Cántico*. Third enlarged edition. Litoral. Mexico City, 1945. 412 pp.
4. *Cántico*. Fourth enlarged edition. First complete edition. Editorial Sudamericana. Buenos Aires, 1950. 540 pp.
4a. *Cántico*. Second complete edition. Editorial Sudamericana. Buenos Aires, 1962. 540 pp.
5. Paul Valéry. *El cementerio marino*. Translated by Jorge Guillén. With drawings by Gino Severini engraved in wood by Pierre Dubreuil. Agrupación de amigos del libro de arte. Madrid-Paris-Buenos Aires, 1930. 25 pp.
6. *Antología*. "Poesia II, 2." Edition by Manuel Altolaguirre. Paris, 1930. 16 pp.
7. *Ardor*. A loose leaf printed by Manuel Altolaguirre. Paris, 1931.
8. *Paso a la aurora*. Edition by Herbert Steiner. Aurora. New York, 1944. 18 pp.
9. *Variaciones sobre temas de Jean Cassou*. Gráfica Panamericana. Mexico City, 1951. 43 pp.
10. *La partida de baile*. With three drawings by Matías Goeritz. Ediciones Espacios. Mexico City, 1951.

11. *El encanto de las sirenas*. With illustrations by Adolfo Halty. Mexico City, 1953. 41 pp.

12. *Huerto de Melibea*. Insula. Madrid, 1954. 27 pp.

13. *Luzbel desconcertado*. Scheiwiller. Milan, 1956. 46 pp.

14. *Del amanecer y el despertar*. Edition by Francisco Pino. Valladolid, 1956. 15 pp.

15. *Clamor: I. Maremágnum*. Editorial Sudamericana. Buenos Aires, 1957. 203 pp.

16. *La Venus de Itálica*. Edition by Maria Victoria Atencia and Rafael León. Málaga, 1957. 6 pp.

17. *Lugar de Lázaro*. Imprenta Dardo. Málaga, 1957. 54 pp.

18. *Viviendo y otros poemas*. Seix Barral. Barcelona, 1958. 110 pp.

19. *El abanico de Solita*. Private edition of 7 copies. Cambrige, Mass., 1960. 4 pp.

20. *Historia natural*. Papeles de Son Armadans. Madrid-Palma de Mallorca, 1960. 91 pp.

21. *Clamor: II. . . . Que van a dar en la mar*. Editorial Sudamericana. Buenos Aires, 1960. 201 pp.

22. *Anita*. Edition by Javier Sologuren. Lima, 1961. 21 pp.

23. *Flores*. Edition by Francisco Sabadell. Valladolid, 1961. 12 pp. (and seven woodcuts).

24. *La niña y la muerte. Ruinas al sol*. "Hojas," no. 9. Bogotá, 1961. 2 pp.

25. *Según las horas*. Editorial de la Universidad de Puerto Rico. Río Piedras, 1962. 49 pp.

26. *Las tentaciones de Antonio*. Edition by Pablo Beltrán de Heredia. Santander, 1962. 29 pp.

27. *Clamor: III. A la altura de las circunstancias*. Editorial Sudamericana. Buenos Aires, 1963. 178 pp.

28. *Suite italienne*. Scheiwiller. Milan, 1964. 45 pp.

28a. *Suite italienne*. Second enlarged edition. Edition by José Luis Plaza. Officina Bodoni. Verona, 1968. 82 pp.

29. *Tréboles*. La isla de los ratones. Santander, 1964. 82 pp.

30. *Selección de poemas*. Gredos. Madrid, 1965. 294 pp.

31. *El trasnochador.* Private facsimile edition of 12 copies. Málaga, 1967. 8 pp.
32. *Homenaje.* Scheiwiller. Milan, 1967. 630 pp.
33. *Poemas de Castilla.* Edition by Julián Calvo. Santiago de Chile, 1968. 52 pp.
34. *Aire Nuestro: Cántico, Clamor, Homenaje.* Scheiwiller. Milan, 1968. 1698 pp.

b. *Prose*

35. *Federico en persona.* Essay (semblanza) and correspondence. Emecé. Buenos Aires, 1959. 143 pp.
36. *El argumento de la obra.* Scheiwiller. Milan, 1961. 43 pp.
37. *Lenguaje y poesía.* Algunos casos españoles. Revista de Occidente. Madrid, 1962. 269 pp.

c. *Translations Into Other Languages*

38. *Lobgesang.* In Auswahl übertragen von Ernst Robert Curtius. Arche Verlag. Zurich, 1952. 79 pp.
39. *Antologia lirica.* Testi editi e inediti, versione e introduzione a cura di Juana Granados. Instituto Editoriale Cisalpino. Milan-Varese, 1955. 230 pp.
40. *Fragments d'un Cantique.* Poèmes traduits de l'espagnol par Roger Asselineau, Jean Cassou, Pierre Darmangeat, Jules Supervielle, Paul Verdevoye. Pierre Seghers. Paris, 1956. 85 pp.
41. *Jorge Guillén.* Tradotto da Eugenio Montale. Scheiwiller. Milan, 1958. 35 pp.
42. Darius Milhaud. *Poèmes de Jorge Guillén.* Pour chœurs mixtes a capella. Heugel et Cie. Paris, 1958. 38 pp.
43. *Federico in persona.* Carteggio. Versione dallo spagnolo di Margherita Guidacci. Scheiwiller. Milan, 1960. 205 pp.
44. *La fuente.* Variazioni su di un tema di Romano Bilenchi. Versione di Mario Luzi. Scheiwiller. Milan, 1961. 27 pp.
45. *Language and Poetry.* Some Poets of Spain. Harvard University Press. Cambridge, Mass., 1961. 293 pp.

46. *Berufung zum Sein*. Ausgewählte Gedichte ins Deutsche übertragen von Hildegard Baumgardt. Limes Verlag. Wiesbaden,
1963. 116 pp.

47. *Tres epigramas*. Versión de Vanni Scheiwiller. Edition by Rafael León. Málaga, 1964. 4 pp.

48. *Cántico: A Selection*. Edited by Norman Thomas Di Giovanni.
An Atlantic Monthly Press Book. Little, Brown & Co. Boston-
Toronto,/André Deutsch. London, 1965. 291 pp.

49. *Mein Freund Federico García Lorca*. Limes Verlag. Wiesbaden,
1965. 156 pp.

50. *Sprache und Poesie*. Einige Beispiele aus Spanien. Carl Hanser
Verlag. München, 1965. 219 pp.

51. *Affirmation*. A bilingual anthology, 1919–1966. Edited and translated by Julian Palley. University of Oklahoma Press. Norman,
Okla., 1968. 208 pp.

Jorge Guillén in *Books Abroad* 1929–69

The first item in this bibliography is a perspicacious review of the 1928 edition of *Cántico* by Erasmo Buceta. We reprint it here in its entirety, since it has lost little of its validity in the forty years that have passed.

It was in Valladolid, the city which at the beginning of the seventeenth century was not only the court of Spain but also of the poets—the city in which at one stage of his career Góngora dwelt, making it the butt of his gibes—that Guillén was born. He studied in Madrid, living in the same place, the old Residencia de Estudiantes, as did one of the most renowned figures among contemporary Spanish lyricists, Juan Ramón Jiménez. After taking his doctorate, Guillén went as "lecturer" to the Sorbonne, coming into contact with the greatest French poet of today, Paul Valéry.

To these figures may be traced his spiritual ancestry—a glorious galaxy, in truth, of finesse, purity, aristocracy; representative of an art refined, recondite, poetically supreme. All three, all four of these men, could sponsor that revealing Horatian phrase: *"Non ego ventosae plebis suffragia venor."* Such was the impression one might glean from Guillén's previous work and his latest beautifully done volume—the work of the now professor of Spanish literature in the University of Murcia—marks the ascendancy of these same principles.

The intelligent French critic, Jean Cassou, affirms that the book *"constitue un de ces miracles, de ces points insoutenables où le concret et l'abstrait, le chaud et le froid, l'ombre et la lumière se marient de la façon la plus parfaite."* (*Les Nouvelles Littéraires* of June 1, 1929).

He is right. Guillén's poetry is paradoxical in its fusion of simplicity and complexity, possessing the precision of a clear-cut precious stone coupled with the beat of palpitating flesh, the unbending directness of the straight line with the charming curve of a breeze-swept branch. Can chromatic wealth be perceived in a canvas of dead-white media? This is the sensitized impression resulting from Guillén's unparalleled intellectual imagery.

1) *Cántico* (Madrid. Revista de Occidente, 1928), reviewed by Erasmos Buceta in *BA* 3:4, p. 374 (see above).

2) *La poética de Bécquer* (New York. Hispanic Institute. 1943), reviewed by Willis Knapp Jones in *BA* 19:3, p. 284.

3) *Cántico*, 3rd ed. (México. Litoral. 1945), reviewed by Aubrey F. G. Bell in *BA* 20:4, p. 394.

4) *Lobgesang* (Zürich. Arche. 1952. Ernst Robert Curtius, tr.), reviewed by Herbert Steiner in *BA* 28:1, pp. 32–33.

5) *Huerto de Melibea* (Madrid. Insula. 1954), reviewed by Bernice G. Duncan in *BA* 31:4, p. 371.

6) *Viviendo y otros poemas* (Barcelona. Seix Barral. 1958), reviewed by Ivar Ivask in *BA* 34:1, p. 25.

7) *Clamor* II: . . . *Que van a dar en la mar* (Buenos Aires. Sudamericana. 1960), reviewed by Ivar Ivask in *BA* 36:1, pp. 63–64.

8) *Language and Poetry: Some Poets of Spain* (Cambridge, Mass. Harvard University Press. 1961), reviewed by Ivar Ivask in *BA* 36:2, pp. 208–209.

9) *El argumento de la obra* (Milan. Scheiwiller. 1961), reviewed by Ivar Ivask in *BA* 36:3, pp. 300–301.

10) *Clamor* III: *A la altura de las circunstancias* (Buenos Aires. Sudamericana. 1963) and *Según las horas* (San Juan, P.R. Editorial Universitaria. 1962), reviewed by Ivar Ivask in *BA* 38:3, p. 296.

11) *Selección de poemas* (Madrid. Gredos. 1965) and *Cántico: A Selection* (Boston, Little, Brown. 1965. Norman Thomas di Giovanni, ed.), reviewed by Ivar Ivask in *BA* 41:1, p. 78.

12) *Homenaje* (Milan. Scheiwiller, 1967), reviewed by Ivar Ivask in *BA* 42:1, pp. 7–12.

13) "An International Symposium in Honor of Jorge Guillén at 75," in *BA* 42:1, pp. 7–60.

14) *Suite italienne* (Verona. Officina Bodoni, 1968), reviewed by Ivar Ivask in *BA* 42:4, p. 558.

15) *Aire Nuestro* (Milan. Scheiwiller, 1968), reviewed by Ivar Ivask in *BA* 43:2, p. 236.

The text for *Luminous Reality* has been set on the Linotype in eleven-point Granjon, with two points of space added between lines for added readability. One of England's great printers, George W. Jones, designed Granjon to meet his own exacting requirements for fine book and publication work, and it remains today one of the many fine typefaces for the letterpress printing of books.

The paper on which this book was printed bears the watermark of the University of Oklahoma Press and has an intended effective life of at least three hundred years.